EXCITEMENT FOR MULTIPLYING MOVEMENTS

Forge has developed Multiplying Movements *at the most opportune time in the life of the Global Church. According to recent research, church leadership is now focusing on the "greatest gap" in church ministry: "Discipleship." Uniquely, Forge has developed and is providing this reproductive, ministry-wide tool, now available to all evangelists and other Great Commission networks, a systemic, full-Gospel approach, biblically relevant, practical, easily implemented and led in community.*

—Tom Phillips, Senior Advisor, Billy Graham Evangelistic Association

Brother Charlie and his four-generational Christian household are spiritual role models—full of vigor and vitality—who have served the Lord as wind spreads a wildfire. With sharp insight bestowed by the Holy Spirit, Brother Charlie conveys concepts for the growth of the Heavenly Kingdom through grassroots movements. After reading these twelve profound chapters, it was akin to unlocking twelve doors to start the cycle of multiplying laborer movements, which brings a refreshing perspective, as if basking in a gentle spring breeze. May the Lord use this book to bring about a great spiritual revival.

—Peter and Ruth Xu Yong Ze, Founder & Leaders of the Born Again Movement, An Underground Chinese House Church Network Furthering the *Back to Jerusalem* Vision

Multiplying Movements *is a powerful and timely resource that stirred both my heart and vision for making disciples who live on mission. It's deeply convicting and refreshingly clear—reminding me that true Kingdom impact begins with personal devotion and obedience to God and His Word. This isn't just a book to read; it's one to get stirred up by and apply. I walked away renewed, challenged to let Scripture shape every layer of my leadership and life. If you care about making disciples who make disciples, this resource will equip and inspire you to lead with purpose and clarity. Don't just read it—let it move you to further dependence upon the Lord and to be a laborer in the field who is advancing God's Kingdom.*

— Jason Mick, Next Gen Pastor, Prestonwood Baptist Church, Plano, TX

Multiplying Movements *captures a profound biblical truth that can transform how we live and disciple others. From the very beginning, God's heart has been to fill the earth with people who know, love, and walk with Him—and He invites us to join Him in that mission. This book is deeply spiritual and intensely practical, offering wisdom and application for every believer eager to fulfill God's purpose by multiplying disciples. The insights here have reshaped my ministry, and I'm convinced they will inspire and equip you as well. If you long to grow as a disciple and disciple-maker, see disciples multiplied, and God's kingdom expanded, then* Multiplying Movements *is a must-read!*

— Sammy Tippit, Sammy Tippit Ministries Founder and Author of *God's Secret Agent*

With vivid storytelling and heartfelt passion, Multiplying Movements *offers a simple yet powerful guide to disciple-making. Written with clarity and biblical conviction, it is especially valuable for new believers eager to grow and get involved in God's mission right away. Packed with practical questions and grounded in real-life application, this book moves beyond inspiration to instigation of Great Commission work.*

—Dr. David E. Bosworth, Professor of New Testament Studies and Mission, Colorado Christian University

Multiplying Movements *is exactly what this generation—desperate for a real move of God—needs. We can't afford to miss this moment. This resource isn't just helpful; it's essential. It will move believers from consumers to contributors, and the impact will be undeniable.*

— Britton Bishop, Youth Pastor, Church on the Move, Tulsa, OK

Charlie Marq's Multiplying Movements *book is one of the best resources available for practically fulfilling the Great Commission and equipping others to become Kingdom Laborers. What stands out to me is that the words on these pages are not just theories, ideas, or strategies—these are biblical truths that Charlie lives out every day with consistency and passion. His personal commitment to making disciples adds authenticity and weight to every page.*

—Caleb McNaughton, Lead Pastor, Highpoint Church, Aurora, CO

In this day and time we are living in, with a harvest that is so plentiful, I can hardly think of better information to sow into your hearts and minds than Multiplying Movements! *The fire of the Gospel needs to spread to all the world and* Multiplying Movements *is the type of resource needed to help you do just that! Praise the Lord for Charlie Marq along with the Forge team, whose hearts are on fire for the Gospel!*

—Derek Gaskill, Former Player for the New York Mets, Toronto Blue Jays, and Milwaukee Brewers; Pro Baseball Instructor; & Evangelist

This book should be in the hands of every movement leader, trainer, and mobilizer in the world. It brings needed clarity and unity to a global movement effort. If I were to recommend just one book to someone who wants to understand and be part of the global movements God is igniting, this would be it.

—Brandon Harrison, Student Pastor, Shandon Baptist Church, Columbia, SC

Multiplying Movements *is more than a resource—it's a wake-up call to the Church. It gives language to many believers' ache: "I want to make a difference, but I don't know where to start." Charlie and the team at Forge have created something powerful, practical, Spirit-led, and deeply rooted in the mission of Jesus. This is a must-read if you long to see ordinary people become everyday disciple-makers.*

— Peter Reeves, Founder, Reeves Initiative

This book is full of practical tools and passionate guidance to help move someone from a new believer to a committed laborer for Christ. The application questions are especially helpful for encouraging readers to live and love like Jesus right where they are at. I'd highly recommend this to any youth leader looking to disciple their students in a meaningful and intentional way.

—Ben Worley, Student Pastor, Revive Church, Arvada, CO

Multiplying Movements *is a stirring and essential invitation to every Christ-follower: mission isn't reserved for a select few—it's the heartbeat of the Gospel and the calling of us all. With bold clarity and Spirit-filled urgency, this book reframes "sent-ness" not as an occasional act, but as a lifestyle—one where Jesus radiates from our very being into every corner of our lives. More than just a call to live on mission, it equips and inspires you to multiply that mission in others, unleashing waves of disciple-making that echo across generations. If you're ready to live with deeper purpose and catalyze lasting Kingdom impact, this book is your guide.*

— Jesse Kroeze, Executive Director, Touch The World & The Missions Academy

MULTIPLYING MOVEMENTS WORKBOOK

FORGE

Multiplying Movements Workbook

Full Book ISBN 978-1-7358775-1-8 (Paperback)
Full Book ISBN 978-1-7358775-4-9 (eBook)
Workbook ISBN 979-8-9866057-6-0 (Paperback)
Workbook ISBN 979-8-9866057-7-7 (eBook)

Requests to use material contained in this publication should be in writing to: Publisher, Forge 14485 East Evans Avenue, Denver, Colorado 80014.

Cover Design by Lauren Atherton and Stephanie Andersson.

Written by Forge.

Visit us online at www.ForgeForward.org

CONTENTS

HOW TO ACCESS MULTIPLYING MOVEMENTS VIDEOS

CORRESPONDING VIDEOS

This workbook is specifically designed for use alongside the Multiplying Movements 12-part video series. You can find the accompanying videos for each chapter on the Forge App at **TheForgeApp.com** or at **MultiplyingMovements.com.**

If you would prefer to study Multiplying Movements in written format instead of video, it is also available as a separate, stand-alone book. The full book is available for purchase at **MultiplyingMovements.com** and can be used without need for the workbook and videos, depending on personal preference.

A few notes on how to watch:

- In the interactive Forge app on your phone or tablet, click the "Multiplying Movements" box and you will be able to view all the videos **full screen** by clicking the expansion icon in the right corner once the video appears.

- On your <u>computer</u> web browser (not your phone or tablet), go to MultiplyingMovements.com and click "Try Web Version." The link will take you to a page that has a QR Code on the left (for putting the app on your phone or tablet) and a picture of a phone on the right. The phone, however, is so much more than a picture—it's a fully functional app you can interact with and play the videos from on your computer (click it and see!).

- Lastly, the web version of the app can be accessed from a phone or tablet in addition to a computer. Just know that on a phone or tablet, the web version will function like a normal app.

FOREWORD BY DESMOND HENRY

Movements are not born in boardrooms and do not always emanate from exceptional strategic plans. They are often born in brokenness, prayer, and obedience—when everyday people say "yes" to Jesus in the ordinary rhythms of life. *Multiplying Movements* is not merely a discipleship resource—it is a launching pad for mobilizing Kingdom Laborers across every corner of society globally. This is not theory. This is how transformation has always worked.

As a missiologist, I have spent my life studying what ignites real, lasting Gospel movements—from the explosive disciple-making underground churches of Southeast Asia to the grassroots revival stirring on the African soil to Spirit-led networks rising among Gen Z in post-Christian cities. There is a pattern: simple obedience, reproducible, scalable methods, and Spirit-empowered multiplication. This is a theme that resonates deeply with Scripture itself.

This book captures that pattern. And it does so not from the voice of a distant academic, or thought leaders in air conditioned offices, but from the lived experiences of men and women who have walked among the lost, wept over the invisible, and dared to believe that Jesus meant what He said in Matthew 9: "The harvest is plentiful, but the laborers are few."

A RESOURCE THAT BUILDS LABORERS—AND MOVEMENTS

Multiplying Movements is built around a gradual, intentional structure that reflects the journey of disciple to disciple-maker to movement catalyst. The content is neither abstract nor idealistic—it is grounded in gritty stories, clear action steps, and spiritual disciplines shaped by biblical conviction. It is a tool forged in the field and written with practitioners in mind.

Each chapter walks the reader deeper—from personal intimacy with God to practical habits of sharing Jesus with others. You are not just reading concepts; you are being trained, equipped, and commissioned. And when the final chapter comes, it does not end with a bow. It ends with a baton.

The final section, *Your Next Steps: Multiplying the Movement*, drives home a critical truth: this is not a course you complete; it is a calling you continue. The reader is not only invited to reflect but is actively sent—commissioned to be the laborer Jesus asked us to pray for in Matthew 9:38. They are called to spiritual reproduction, to disciple-making, and to Kingdom impact that multiplies far beyond themselves.

And with tools like *The Laborer's Declaration*, the reader is invited to declare—daily—that their life belongs to the King and His mission. Not one chapter is disconnected from this greater movemental purpose. This is practical theology at its best.

WHY THIS RESOURCE MATTERS NOW

We live in a moment of global shaking—a tumultuous moment that does not change the mission we are on. Church attendance is declining in some regions, while Gospel hunger explodes in others. In every context—urban, rural, digital, or diaspora—the one common need is this: more Kingdom Laborers.

Not more spectators. Not more professionals. But more everyday believers who live sent lives. Jesus' answer to the world's pain was people filled with His Spirit, living as His presence in the world. This book gets that. It trains people for that. And it launches people into that life.

If you're a church leader, this book gives you a reproducible discipleship engine. If you're a new believer, it gives you direction and clarity. If you're a stagnant Christian, it gives you a fire. And if you're ready to disciple others, it gives you a roadmap.

ONE LIFE THAT MULTIPLIES

In Isaiah 51:2, God reminds His people, "When I called [Abraham] he was only one man, and I blessed him and made him many" (NIV). That is the story of every true movement. One person. One obedient step. One "yes" to Jesus. And from that, the Spirit of God multiplies what only He can.

Multiplying Movements is a tool to shape those Abrahams. It is a spark to light fires in living rooms, workplaces, cafés, and campuses. It is how ordinary people get activated for extraordinary mission.

So, here's my encouragement to you: don't just read this book. Respond to it. Let it take root in you. Share it. Teach it. Multiply it. Because the prayer request of Jesus is still unanswered in many places. And maybe you are one of His answers.

"The harvest is plentiful, but the laborers are few. Therefore, pray earnestly to the Lord of the harvest to send out laborers into His harvest." — Matthew 9:37–38, ESV

Let's not just pray for laborers. Let's become them. Let's not just hope for movements. Let's multiply them.

The best is yet to come.

Desmond Henry, PhD

Missiologist

International Director, Palau, Global Network of Evangelists

DON'T MISS THIS: YOUR LAUNCH INTO THE MULTIPLYING MOVEMENTS VISION

By Charlie Marq

Have you ever wondered, *What is the greatest need in the entire world?* I have often wondered this question. Is it starvation? People who do not have enough food or enough nutrition. Is it a lack of clean water? Is it health issues? People around the world with bad healthcare access, who are struggling and dying daily. Is it sex trafficking? Modern-day slaves living day after day with no one to rescue them. Is it people dying without hope? What is it?

What is the greatest need in the entire world?

The greatest need in the world was unveiled to me when I spoke with three different people from various places across the globe in one week—and they all pointed to this one, great need.

A believer in South Asia declared on the phone, "Listen, Charlie, there are a lot of suffering people all around us. But there is one great problem. . ."

That same week, another believer in remote Himalayan regions of Asia urgently shared, "Charlie, there are remote people all over and they are suffering right now. They are helpless! But there is one massive issue. . ."

Again that week, my phone buzzed. I received a message from a ministry partner in East Africa stating, "Charlie, there are a lot of villages with people in great need. But there is one huge need. . ."

In each of those conversations, the greatest need in the entire world became clearer to me.

Now, while this great need certainly exists in countries all over the globe, it is clearly in my own backyard too. One time, I was walking around the downtown area of my city, and I saw a homeless man holding a cardboard sign that read: "Need Shoes."

Approaching the man, I said, "I'm Charlie. What is your name?"

"I'm Willis."

Willis towered over me like the skyscrapers behind him. Since I am a whopping 5 feet, 5 inches tall, it struck me that we must have looked like David and Goliath. I said, "Willis, my shoes won't fit you. But I want to ask you something: Do you know anything about Jesus?"

Without warning, Willis began belligerently screaming. Worse yet, he was screaming *at me!* "I hate you Christians!" he shouted. "Get out of my face! Go away before I beat you!"

While this probably wasn't the wisest idea, I thought, *why not stick around for a few more minutes and see if the conversation goes any further?*

It did not.

As I walked away, Willis furrowed his brow in fury, accusing me with pain-filled words that I will never forget: "You Christians are always walking by me, but you won't even look at me!"

That statement struck me to my core and convicted me deeply. As I thought about it throughout the rest of the day, I prayerfully wondered,

Lord, how many people have I passed by without really seeing them? How many people have I ignored or failed to even notice? How many people have I simply not cared about? How many people have I been too busy for?"

This is nothing like Jesus. No. Jesus did not just pass by people like Willis. Jesus *saw* each person. Matthew 9:36 says, "When [Jesus] *saw* the crowds, He had compassion for them" (ESV, emphasis mine). He took note of them. He observed their deepest needs and moved in closer to engage them. And in the midst of this, Jesus looks at His disciples and says, "The harvest is plentiful . . ." There is a lot of work to be done. ". . . but the laborers are few" (Matthew 9:37, ESV). There are not enough people to get the work done.

Do you know what those three people who called me all declared? "There is one great problem: there are not enough people to do the work! There are not enough laborers!"

There are unending physical and spiritual needs to be met. But there are not enough people to carry the heart and the message of Jesus to meet those needs.

Our world is in desperate need of more Kingdom Laborers.

Not only is this the greatest need in the world—because it is the need behind all needs—but it is simultaneously the greatest *solution* to the greatest need. We need more people to get out into harvest fields, and to become the laborers God is calling them to become! People like *you*!

I travel a lot and meet all sorts of people. And I often find that even strong believers say things like, "I want to make an impact. I want to labor for God's Kingdom. I want to share Jesus with others and make disciples. I know I should, but, how? I do not know what to do. What should I do next?" Maybe you have felt that way too. Or maybe you just want to grow in Christ and take your next step. Wherever you are, this discipleship pathway is for you!

This is why *Multiplying Movements* exists: to help answer the world's greatest need—to help you become a laborer for God's Kingdom as one who loves Jesus, loves others, and advances His Kingdom every day, everywhere. You can be the difference our world needs! You live in harvest fields no one else does. You have the opportunity to live a world-changing life of impact!

Too often we have been under-challenged, over-entertained, and ill-equipped. So, buckle up! While I believe *Multiplying Movements* is quite entertaining, it will go far beyond entertainment. This tool will challenge you to your core, practically equip you to change the world, and radically change your life!

BEFORE YOU GO FURTHER, HERE ARE A FEW CRUCIAL THINGS FOR YOU TO KNOW:

1. **Connecting with the Greater Multiplying Movements Community and Network**: This *Multiplying Movements* discipleship pathway is intentionally designed to have the greatest impact when shared with others! We want to support you and connect you with a Laborership community where you can ask questions, share prayer needs, and receive pertinent elements and updates as you go through *Multiplying Movements*! Register using the QR code on the next page right now at **MultiplyingMovements.com** so we can pray for you and connect you with additional resources as you step forward into the wider Forge Family! This will be critical for your journey—whether you are personally going through *Multiplying Movements* for the first time or taking others through it.

2. **Engaging Someone to Come Alongside You or Coming Alongside Others**: If an individual has not invited you to engage in the *Multiplying Movements* journey, but you received it some other way, be sure to find someone in your church or in your community who is farther down the trail of faith than you are who might be able to come alongside your faith journey. Before digging into the full chapters, ask that person, "Would you be willing to go through *Multiplying Movements* with me to help me grow spiritually as we do? I would love to learn from your life and engage this discipleship tool together." As you meet, honestly engage the discussion questions together. The *Tips for Coming Alongside a Person or Small Group* **section in Appendix A** will be important for them to review before you meet together. This section will also eventually become important for you, as God may begin to ignite and encourage others through your life as you engage the fullness of *Multiplying Movements*. Or, if you are picking up *Multiplying Movements* for the first time to come alongside others or take a small group through it, then please read through Appendix A beforehand as well for tips on using this resource with others.

3. **"Now What?"**: You will find questions and journaling space titled "Now What" after every chapter—use these sections to prayerfully process, and to write notes as God is growing you.

Your true spiritual growth will come as you process these sections and take action, stepping out in obedience to Jesus!

4. **Building on the Foundation**: As you dig in, you will notice Chapter One lays out the vision of becoming a laborer for God's Kingdom. At this point, you might be wondering, *What does that even look like?* Chapter One will help you understand what a Kingdom Laborer is and cast vision for who God is calling us to become as laborers. After you catch the vision of Kingdom Laborership, Chapter Two will be the starting line, launching you into the first step for developing *a heart on fire* for Jesus, and every chapter will build forward from that foundation.

5. **Made to Multiply**: We will never see movements multiplied unless we encourage others, investing in them what we have received. While everything you receive in *Multiplying Movements* is for you, it's not only for you!

As you progress through this organic and relational, yet directionally-focused discipleship process, you will eventually be equipped to come alongside others using this tool, passing to them what God has given you—whether that is other believers who need this tool to become laborers who change their world too, or others that you lead to Christ. In 2 Timothy 2:2 Paul the Apostle writes to Timothy and says, "And the things you have heard me say . . . entrust to reliable people who will also be qualified to teach others" (NIV). In this passage we see a movement birthed through life-on-life spiritual multiplication. Paul passed to Timothy what he had received and challenged Timothy to go and do the same. This is how more laborers can be raised up to meet the vast needs of the entire world, carrying the love and message of Jesus to those who desperately need Him.

Right now, if you are feeling inadequate and thinking *There is no way I can do this! I do not have what it takes.* Don't worry! You don't need to be able to do this yet. You will be surprised by how much God grows you, equips you, and puts this very desire in you as you engage Him and others in this process of becoming a world-changing Kingdom Laborer!

Let's get started! Right now, will you ask God to help you grow into a Kingdom Laborer who loves Jesus, loves others, and advances His Kingdom every day, everywhere?

Again, you might be thinking, *I do not have the capacity or the ability,* and that is okay! At this point, that does not matter. God can provide you with the training and framework you need to become a Kingdom Laborer, impacting your spheres of influence—and He can do it through *Multiplying Movements*! You may not be a laborer yet, but you are beginning the growth process to get there. Or maybe you are, but you want to continue being sharpened in your impact. Either way, what matters most right now is your willingness to say "yes" to Jesus and His Kingdom cause.

What if—right here, right now, today—your life began to fulfill the prayer request of Jesus (Matthew 9:38) by simply starting the journey to becoming a Kingdom Laborer through *Multiplying Movements*? We'll walk you through each step, so that by the time you finish for the first time, you will already be living as a laborer (and even ready to multiply the movement by bringing along others into the process too —whether one-on-one or launching a group of your own)!

WHAT SHOULD I DO NEXT?

Years ago as I traveled the globe witnessing people coming to Christ, and began equipping them to grow spiritually and become Laborers for the Kingdom, they too began leading others to follow Jesus, who in turn did the same! Movements began! It was thrilling, but I became deeply concerned with questions like: *How can I be sure they will remain firm following Jesus? How do I know that the people they lead to Christ will not veer off the path of truth? How do I know the movement will remain pure as Jesus desires?*

These questions led me to seek out mentors, learn from wiser world-changing followers of Christ, and to research the most revolutionary discipleship models with long-lasting impact. After much wrestling, trial by fire in the field, too many mistakes, and a good number of spiritual victories too, *Multiplying Movements* emerged.

With God's help, we have attempted to take the best from concepts like disciple-making movements, discovery Bible studies, training for trainers, and more, merging them into one tool fused with the DNA of Forge—God empowering every ordinary person for extraordinary impact in every facet and sphere of society worldwide. And now, not only has this discipleship tool greatly impacted nations worldwide, but it has been put in your hands to advance His Kingdom cause in your life and spheres of influence.

YOUR PRAYER COMMITMENT

Today, I commit to asking God to grow me into His everyday, everywhere Kingdom Laborer as I engage the *Multiplying Movements* discipleship tool:

Signature: _____ Date: _____

DISCUSSION

1. Each person briefly share your story (highlighting how you met Jesus, what your life was like before giving your life to Jesus, and what brought you to where you are today). Be open and honest as you share, knowing each of you are not here to impress anyone but to grow. Conclude with sharing what you hope God will do in your life as a result of going through *Multiplying Movements* together.
2. Pray together.

YOU'RE NOT ALONE

We want to support you and come alongside you as you journey through Multiplying Movements! Tell us about your group at **MultiplyingMovements.com** so we can pray for you and connect you with additional resources.

We'll give you (and each person you come alongside) access to more Forge Resources, crucial updates, and encouragement in the journey! You will also get to continue being part of the greater Multiplying Movements Laborership Community and Forge Family where you can ask questions, share prayer needs, and connect with other Kingdom Laborers.

We pray you are equipped and encouraged through Multiplying Movements to impact your every day, everywhere spheres of influence as a Kingdom Laborer in the "harvest fields" God places you. And may God empower you to multiply countless others for theirs!

1

THE VISION: BECOMING EVERYDAY, EVERYWHERE KINGDOM LABORERS

Matthew 9:35-38 • Matthew 20:28 • Ephesians 5:1-2

**Do you want your life
to make an _____ on this world?**

Jesus was focused on seeking and saving the lost, and His strategic plan was more Kingdom Laborers in every facet and sphere of society worldwide!

JESUS' MINISTRY MODEL & STRATEGY:

Up-_____

You may impress up front, from a distance. But you impact up-close.

"The harvest is plentiful" (Matthew 9:35-38)—there are too many people without hope and without purpose. There is a lot of work to be done, so pray for more harvest hands!

In the _____ of everyday life

Outside the synagogue/church: workplaces, recreation locations, where you live.

One _____ at a time

Domino-ripple effect... More time with less people causes greater impact.

JESUS' MINISTRY METHOD:

_____ – Take note of the people around you.

_____ – Slow down enough to truly engage others.

_____ _____ _____ – Life transformation often happens when we spend time with others life-on-life, up-close. This often happens at meal tables!

Love is spelled ___ ___ ___ ___.

A KINGDOM LABORER IS SOMEONE WHO...

- Strategically follows Jesus' method of impacting others.

- Sees, Stops, and Spends time with others.

- Loves God with everything and loves others, 24/7 every day and everywhere.

YOUR OBSTACLES

"I'm too imperfect."

We don't need to look to ourselves, but rather just need to point to the One who is _____!

"My sin struggle has disqualified me. I'm too unworthy."

You have not lost your value to God. Welcome to the unworthy club; He is the _____ one!

"I don't have enough knowledge."

Has Jesus shown up for you? If so, you have _____-_____ to tell. Jesus has worked through ordinary people time and time again! (Acts 4:13)

"I'm too afraid."

Pray the Ten-Finger prayer: "I can do all things through _____ who strengthens me."

NOW WHAT?

Write down your prayer commitment to God here (something like "Lord, I commit to becoming a laborer for your Kingdom. I trust You are shaping my life, and I desire to make the lasting impact you designed me for!").

COMMIT TO BECOMING A KINGDOM LABORER:

Starting this week, where can you begin to see, stop, and spend time with people?

What are your potential obstacles? List them here and talk to God about them:

Go back through your obstacles above and write God's truth next to each one to help you overcome.

BEGIN MEMORIZING THE MEMORY VERSE:

————————————————————————————————

". . .The harvest is plentiful, but the laborers are few." — Matthew 9:37, ESV

————————————————————————————————

WHAT IF . . . ?

Are there others who have come alongside your life and helped you to get where you are today in your spiritual life? Write down their names here:

Pause now and thank God for these people and their willingness to spend time encouraging you in your spiritual growth, realizing you likely wouldn't be where you are today if it wasn't for them!

Are there people in your life who need that same kind of encouragement? Do you imagine their lives being impacted in the same way if someone would come alongside them too? Write down a few of their names here:

Begin to pray for them now. As you pray, be encouraged—Kingdom Laborers are not perfect people; including those who have taken the time to come alongside your life. And Kingdom Laborers don't always have all the answers. But they get things done, simply saying yes to Jesus. And, that all begins in prayer!

DISCUSSION

1. Pray together.
2. Review Memory Verse.
3. Read Key Scriptures: Matthew 9:35-38; Matthew 20:28; Ephesians 5:1-2.
4. Review key concepts from the chapter. Share how you are processing and any comments you have. Did anything in particular really resonate with you? Is there anything you disagreed with? Or is there anything you will never forget? Do you have any questions about it?
5. How would our world be affected if there were no physical workers (no food delivery drivers, no factory workers, no construction workers, no road builders, etc.)? Now consider, what if Jesus doesn't have laborers for His Kingdom vs. what would happen if every Christian approached life as God's everyday, everywhere laborer?
6. What are some of your mainstream, everyday places you show up? How can you begin to see, stop, and spend time with people wherever you go?
7. Which obstacles discussed in the chapter (or video) affect you the most?
8. After everyone shares, encourage each other with God's truth from the chapter or episode.
9. Review "What If . . ." Section and the Memory Verse again.
10. Everyone share—what is your one key takeaway or action step for this week?
11. Pray together.

OTHER HELPFUL RESOURCES:

Plan A: And There is No Plan B (Book and Audio) by Dwight Robertson

For purchasing options and more resources, go to: **MultiplyMore.com**

NOTES

The Vision: Becoming Kingdom Laborers

NOTES
The Vision: Becoming Kingdom Laborers

2

THE STARTING PLACE: DEVELOPING A HEART ON FIRE

Matthew 22:37 • Revelation 2:4-5 • John 14:15

**Everyone is in one of four chairs.
The goal is getting in chair ___.**

CHAIR 1: ON FIRE

SOMEONE WHO COMPLETELY AND TOTALLY LOVES _____. (John 14:15, Luke 10:27)

People do crazy things when they are in _____! People around you can tell what you love by the way you act and live.

The person in chair one:

- Reads the _____.
- Spends time praying.
- Shares their faith.
- Is full of the _____ of the Lord, even in suffering and persecution. (Nehemiah 8:10)

CHAIR 2: LUKEWARM

SOMEONE WHO BELIEVES IN JESUS BUT HAS BECOME COMPLACENT.

The person in chair two:

- Has gotten _____ to God.
- Goes half speed for Jesus.
- Is more focused on how they feel than what God thinks of their worship.
- Is self-focused.
- Is hypocritically living in sin but acting differently in church and around other believers.

"You have left your first _____." (Revelation 2:2-4)

How we treat our family reveals what we think about Jesus.

(Ephesians 5:22-6:4)

Chair two is "_____" to Jesus. (Revelation 3:15-20)

CHAIR 3: UNKNOWINGLY LOST

SOMEONE WHO THINKS THEY ARE SAVED BUT ARE NOT.

This chair is the most spiritually dangerous place to be!

The person in chair three:

- Has possibly prayed a prayer, been baptized, or joined a church but they never truly trusted in Christ.
- Is not bothered by their _____; they have no conviction of
  _____.
- Has no spiritual fruit or life change.

CHAIR 4: UNBELIEVER

SOMEONE WHO DOES NOT BELIEVE IN JESUS.

The person in chair four knows for a fact they are not a
_____.

HOW DO YOU GET TO CHAIR ONE?

If you are in chair four: Tell Jesus you are sorry for your sin and give your life to Him!

If you are in chair three: You need to give your life to Jesus. If you are not sure whether you are in chair two or three, then give yourself fully to Jesus and make sure! Tell Jesus, "I am sorry for my sin and I give You everything I am."

If you are in chair two: Tell Jesus, "I want to return to my first love. I am sorry for my sin and I want to re-surrender everything I am to You."

Jesus _____ for us, so we should _____ for Him!

NOW WHAT?

Prayerfully consider which chair you have been in. Write it down here, and why you think that is the chair you have been in:

If you have been in Chair 2, 3, or 4, are you ready to move to Chair 1? If you are, take some time to write a prayer of commitment below. If not, take some time to write out why you are not ready to commit to being a "Chair 1" follower of Jesus.

Take these reasons to God in prayer. We encourage you to make this decision soon—do not wait. Even if you have apprehensions, Jesus can help you through these difficulties.

Write your prayer commitment to Jesus here:

Now, get on your face in prayer declaring your commitment and telling Jesus in your own words, "All I am and all I have is Yours. I give You my entire life."

People who encounter Jesus most often experience some kind of change (such as new peace, joy, freedom from a sin or addiction, hunger for God's Word, etc.). Maybe you experienced some of these changes today while making a commitment to become a "Chair 1" Christian. It is important to remember what God does in our lives!

With that in mind, write down some ways encountering Jesus has changed your life:

Starting this week, what specific next steps can you take to develop your heart on fire for Jesus and continue living in Chair 1?

If you made a commitment to be in Chair 1 today, and have never been baptized before, then we encourage you to find a time to do so. Being baptized is a key step of obedience that Jesus calls us to take when we trust in Him!

If someone led you to fully give your life to Jesus, you might want to ask that person to be the one who baptizes you. If you are part of a local church that has regular baptisms, then we encourage you to speak with your church leadership and get on the baptism schedule. If you need to find a church, consider looking for options using the Billy Graham Evangelistic Association's church locator tool: **Churches. GoingFarther.net.**

Before you get baptized, make sure you have a full understanding of what baptism means:

Baptism is a public declaration that you now identify as a follower of Jesus, that your life of sin has been crucified and put to death with Jesus, and that you are now raised to life with Him and choose to live a new life in Christ. Baptism symbolizes Jesus' death and resurrection, and your life being washed clean of sin. Review Colossians 2:12, Matthew 28:19, and Romans 6:3-4.

BEGIN MEMORIZING THE MEMORY VERSE:

— —

"Love the Lord your God with all your heart, with all your soul, and with all your mind." — Matthew 22:37, NIV

— —

WHAT IF . . . ?

Write down the names of 5-6 people who don't know Jesus yet, people that you'd love to see God ignite their hearts on fire too

(you might know them well or you might not even know their name yet):

Right now, pray for each of them.Will you commit to come back to this list and pray for these people once a week?

DISCUSSION

1. Share any victories or obstacles from last week's action steps.
2. Pray together.
3. Review Memory Verse.
4. Read Key Scriptures: Matthew 22:37; Revelation 2:4-5; John 14:15.
5. Review key concepts from the chapter. Share how you are processing and any comments you have. Did anything in particular really resonate with you? Is there anything you disagreed with? Or is there anything you will never forget? Do you have any questions about it?
6. Before now, what chair do you think you were in, and why? Were you able to surrender all to Jesus, moving to Chair 1?

What was that prayer time like, and do you sense anything is different as a result?

7. Starting this week, what specific next steps will you take to develop your heart on fire for Jesus and continue living in Chair 1?

8. Review "What If . . ." Section and the Memory Verse again.

9. Everyone share—what is your one key takeaway or action step for this week?

10. Pray together.

OTHER HELPFUL RESOURCES:

8 Marks of a Disciple Bible Study (Booklet and Messages) by John Vermilya

For purchasing options and more resources, go to:
MultiplyMore.com

NOTES

The Starting Place: Developing a Heart on Fire

NOTES

The Starting Place: Developing a Heart on Fire

3

SEEKING GOD INTIMATELY

James 4:8 • John 15:5 • Genesis 5:24

**The more _____ I spend with Jesus,
the more I get to _____ Him.**

WALKING WITH GOD

Enoch _____ with God. (Genesis 5:21-24)

In the Bible, the word "walking" is often equivalent to

_____.

You can enjoy fellowship with God anywhere you go, as a lifestyle!

We can _____ God by enjoying fellowship and spending time with Him. (Hebrews 11:5-6)

SEEKING GOD

Rewards of Seeking God:

Getting to _____ God.

Listening to God's Words and understanding His plans. (Jude 1:14-15)

Seeking God through _____:

Read with purpose and expectation.

You can read in chronological order, or read specific books, or search specific topics.

Meditate on and dig into Scripture by asking questions.

Write in your Bible or write on post it notes.

Read with the purpose of getting to know Jesus.

Seeking God through _____:

Come with a list of prayer requests.

Talk to God on the go, all the time, wherever you are, and whatever you are doing.

Enjoying and Worshiping Jesus:

Sit with God, walk with God, hike with God.

Make room to listen for His voice.

Journal what God is doing, your prayers, etc.

Pray out loud.

Praise the Lord and sing to Him.

Spending Extended Time with God through a Day or "Date" Alone with God (DAWG):

Find a location without distractions.

Bring fun snacks (if you are not fasting).

Bring your Bible.

Bring your journal.

Bring worship music.

NOW WHAT?

We often schedule important appointments and times to meet with friends, but we fail to prioritize meeting with God. What if you took some time right now to schedule an EXTENDED Date Alone With God (DAWG)? We promise, you won't regret it!

Write down the date, time, and place you plan to spend time with God:

Date:

Time:

Place:

It is critical to our ongoing spiritual life to spend some time alone with God every day. What time will you daily commit to seeking Jesus? What do you desire your daily time with God to look like?

While it is crucial to spend time alone with God, He goes with us in our daily lives. Starting today, begin to engage and enjoy Jesus throughout your daily on-the-go schedule. **Brainstorm and write down some ways you can remind yourself of God's presence as you go throughout your day:**

BEGIN MEMORIZING THE MEMORY VERSE:

———————————————————————————

"Draw near to God, and He will draw near to you." — James 4:8, CSB

———————————————————————————

WHAT IF . . . ?

Are you where you are in your faith journey because others have come alongside your life? Do you believe those people have prayed for you? Have they encouraged you in certain ways? Have they introduced you to opportunities, resources, or people to help you grow?

Do you believe some of the people in your life need someone to come alongside and encourage them too? Would you be willing to consider being that person for them?

Of the names you wrote down over the last two weeks (in the "What If . . . ?" sections of Chapter 1 and Chapter 2), ask God if there are at least 1-2 of them that you could simply send a message and let them know "I prayed for you today!"

Pray for them and send a message now.

DISCUSSION

1. Share any victories or obstacles from last week's action steps.
2. Pray together.
3. Review Memory Verse.
4. Read Key Scriptures: James 4:8; John 15:5; Genesis 5:24.
5. Review key concepts from the chapter. Share how you are processing and any comments you have. Did anything in particular really resonate with you? Is there anything you disagreed with? Or is there anything you will never forget? Do you have any questions about it?
6. "The greatest gift you will ever give the world is your intimacy with God." How does this truth shift the way you approach your everyday life?
7. When and where are you planning your next extended DAWG?
8. What stops you from regular time with God? How can you improve in daily seeking God?
9. Share your creative ideas to remind yourself of God's presence throughout each day.
10. Review "What If . . ." Section and the Memory Verse again.
11. Everyone share—what is your one key takeaway or action step for this week?
12. Pray together.

OTHER HELPFUL RESOURCES:

Is God Waiting for a Date with You? (Booklet) by Dwight Robertson

Up-Close: A Spiritual Life Notebook to Fuel Your Growth in Christ by Forge

Forged by Fire (Book and Audio) by Dwight Robertson

Practicing God's Presence: Brother Lawrence for Today's Reader by Robert Elmer

For purchasing options and more resources, go to:
MultiplyMore.com

NOTES
Seeking God Intimately

GETTING INTO THE WORD OF GOD

2 Timothy 3:16-17 • Matthew 4:4 • 2 Peter 1:20-21

**What if we committed our lives to learning
God's Word and ways every day?**

WHY WE GET INTO GOD'S WORD

**If God's Word truly became the authority on which we base our
lives:**

**We would grow in firsthand _____ with God, which
brings both joy and awe.**

Too often, we have based our relationship with God primarily
on other people's close relationship with God.

We would learn to hear, know, and _____ His voice.

We follow Jesus in a world of competing _____, so we must seek God's voice based on His Word. (John 10:27)

We must be compelled first by God's _____, then live out our faith based on His truth, and lastly engage emotion only after (not before) His truth!

We must memorize God's Word, allowing it to flow in and through our lives.

HOW WE GET INTO GOD'S WORD

Every time you open the Bible, use the following model in order to dig into the Scripture and allow it to permeate your life...

Practicing Together:
Mark 2:1-12

_____ – **What does the passage say?**
(*What do you learn about God, Jesus, the Holy Spirit, people, sin, evil, etc.*)

_____ – **What is God speaking to you from this passage?**
(*Is something from the passage really jumping out to you? Is there a sin you need to confess, a life example you want to follow, etc.?*)

_____ – **What will you do about it this week?**
(*How can you specifically and practically obey Jesus this week based on what He showed you in the text?*)

_____ – Is there someone you can share this truth with this week?

Is there a verse you should memorize?

TIPS ON GETTING STARTED

- Choose a book of the Bible to read through one passage per day, until you complete that book. Consider starting with the book of Mark as it is the most simple book of the Bible on the life of Jesus. After Mark, dig into Acts to discover how Jesus' followers lived. After Acts, move onto Ephesians to fully comprehend the Gospel message and who we are called to be as followers of Jesus. After Ephesians, continue to read various books of the Bible until you have read every single book.

- Use the **Head, Heart, Hands, Feet** model (from above) each time you read so that you fully engage God's Word with your entire life. (James 1:22-25)

- As you read, choose verses and sections to memorize.

- Write down any questions you have about the passages you read and discuss them with a mentor.

- If you can, use a physical, paper copy of the Bible (studies have proven reading physical copies rather than electronic copies increases retention), and write in your Bible: star, underline, draw, highlight etc.

NOW WHAT?

Honestly evaluate your time in the Bible and select where you currently are:

_____ I read the Bible daily.

_____ I read the Bible 4 or more times per week.

_____ I read the Bible 1-3 times per week.

_____ I read the Bible 2 times per month.

_____ I read the Bible 1 time per month or less.

What is getting in the way of you engaging God's Word more often?

Consider this incredible reality: A recent study by the Center for Bible Engagement found that those who read the Bible four or more times a week (compared to those who read the Bible less than four times a week) had significantly decreased loneliness, significantly increased victory over sin struggles (such as anger, bitterness in relationships, pornography, drunkenness, sex outside of marriage, etc.), and significant increases in sharing the Gospel and discipling others.

Pray now and ask, "Lord, will you increase my hunger for Your Word?"

Choose a book of the Bible and on your own, engage the first passage, practicing *Head, Heart, Hands, and Feet* right now. Commit to continuing this practice in your daily time with God.

PASSAGE:

HEAD: What is this passage saying?

(What is the main message? What do I learn about God the Father, Jesus, the Holy Spirit, or people, creation, evil, etc.)?

HEART: What is God speaking to me, or how did this impact me personally?

(What part sticks out to me? What changes do I need to make in my beliefs, attitudes, actions?)

HANDS: This very week, how will I obey what God has shown me?

(What specific next steps will I take?)

FEET: Who will I share with?

(Is there anyone in my life that I need to tell about what I learned to encourage?)

If you have not yet, consider beginning to read through the entire Bible.

We recommend you begin with the book of Mark (the most simple book about the life of Jesus), then the book of Acts (how Jesus' early followers lived), and then Ephesians (the simple Gospel, your identity in Christ, and the spiritual battle we face daily). Then continue to finish the Bible, book by book. You could even use the Bible reading chart in the Forge book *Up-Close: A Spiritual Life Notebook* to help track your reading. And, in case you wondered, no, you do not have to start on page one with Genesis. The Bible is not just one large book; it is a collection of 66 books! Therefore, you can start in any one of those 66 books, as we have recommended.

BEGIN MEMORIZING THE MEMORY VERSE:

————————————————————————

"All Scripture is God-breathed and is useful . . ." — 2 Timothy 3:16a, NIV

————————————————————————

WHAT IF . . . ?

What is one Scripture that has been really impactful to you throughout *Multiplying Movements* so far? Write it down here:

Far more than your personal words or opinions, when you share the living and active Word of God with others, you are sharing a great gift with them!

So, will you now share this verse with someone to encourage them in their faith journey too? Share it with a person or two from your lists over the last several weeks as a text, letter, email, or word of encouragement. Don't delay! Do it today!

Consider briefly sharing how this Scripture has impacted you, and let them know that you have prayed this verse for their life today too!

DISCUSSION

1. Share any victories or obstacles from last week's action steps.
2. Pray together.

3. Review Memory Verse.

4. Read Key Scriptures: 2 Timothy 3:16-17; Matthew 4:4; 2 Peter 1:20-21.

5. Review key concepts from the chapter. Share how you are processing and any comments you have. Did anything in particular really resonate with you? Is there anything you disagreed with? Or is there anything you will never forget? Do you have any questions about it?

6. Where are you currently on evaluating your time in God's Word? What stops you from getting into God's Word more often?

7. How will you specifically continue to get into God's Word and let it shape your life?

8. Review "What If . . . " Section and the Memory Verse again.

9. Everyone share—what is your one key takeaway or action step for this week?

10. Pray together.

OTHER HELPFUL RESOURCES:

Up-Close: A Spiritual Life Notebook to Fuel Your Growth in Christ by Forge (Look for the "Bible Study" Section).

For purchasing options and more resources, go to:
MultiplyMore.com

NOTES
Engaging the Word of God

5

PURSUING EFFECTIVE PRAYER

1 Thessalonians 5:17 • Philippians 4:6-7 • Matthew 6:9-13

Prayer is a lifestyle and a conversation. God wants to move us from being people that pray to becoming people *of* prayer!

"Lord teach us to pray." (Luke 11:1-5)

People of Prayer, Pray Regularly

Jesus often withdrew to pray. (Luke 6:12)

Prayer needs to be _____ regularly.

How to P.R.A.Y.

P_____ – Reminding ourselves of who God is as we tell Him who He is. Praise completes our enjoyment, and lifts us to see from God's perspective.

R_____ – God shines His light into our lives to fully address our hearts, cleansing them from sin and darkness. We must confess our sin and forgive those who have wronged us.

A_____ – Receiving the truth of who God is in our lives, as we seek Him for our needs. Receiving requires asking (James 4:2-3). God desires to bless us with spiritual "riches" in Christ as we ask Him.

Y_____ – "Not my will but Your will be done" (Luke 22:42). Sometimes God will say "no" to things we ask for because He knows what is best, and He has a plan that we do not always know. Yet, we must trust and submit to Him in all things. More than our own plans and desires, we must desire to see Jesus' Kingdom cause occur in and through our lives.

· · ·

When to Pray (James 5:13-18)

- When we experience _____ and hardship.

> *"God whispers to us in our pleasures,*
> *but He screams at us through our pains."*
> – C.S. Lewis

- When everything is going well.

- When we are _____ or weary.

… We are to pray in *all* circumstances! (Ephesians 6:18)

Prayer is not only talking; it also includes listening. This happens through God's Word and also through the Spirit, because we carry God's presence everywhere we go!

People of Prayer, Pray _____

- We can't pray passionately because we don't pray _____.

- If we do not pray specifically, we never really witness God's answer to our prayer.

- When you pray specifically and witness God answer, it builds your _____ and gives God _____ ...

- ... as this happens you will become more passionate in prayer! (Luke 11:5-10)

People of Prayer, Pray in _____

"Elijah was a man just like us"—God answers the specific prayers of ordinary people who pray in faith, believing that God will answer!

Spirit-Led Scripture-Fed Prayer time: Praying the very Word and _____ of God.

- You can stand on faith knowing that what God has said He will do, He will do!

- There are 8,000 promises in God's Word.

- You can hold onto God's promises in prayer, trusting that He will answer!

NOW WHAT?

Take some time to talk with God using the P.R.A.Y. acronym right now. (Praise, Repent, Ask, Yield). Commit to practicing prayer in your daily time with God. And remember, simply put, prayer is conversation with God.

Listening Prayer Tips: Prayer is a conversation that includes both talking and listening. Consider these common ways that we see God speaking to us throughout Scripture.

The Bible: God always communicates to us through the plain meaning of Scripture and also through Scripture penetrating our hearts based on our specific circumstances (2 Timothy 3:16; Psalm 19:10-12).

Whispers: The still small voice of God often comes through a gentle nudge inside, something going off in your spirit like a soft beeping alarm, or thoughts that are not our own but from the Holy Spirit (Mark 13:11; Acts 8:29; Acts 13:2; Acts 20:23).

Images: Dreams as we sleep or visions that we see while awake, almost as if they are in our imagination, can be from God (Acts 16:9-10; Acts 2:17; Acts 10:9-18).

Burdens: You may feel overwhelming compassion, heavy-hearted, or compelled by God that you must do something (Acts 20:22; Jeremiah 20:9; Matthew 9:36; Luke 19:41-46).

Right now, pray, asking the Lord in Jesus' name to silence your flesh and the enemy. Ask God to speak to you and ask that you hear His voice alone. Maybe you have a specific question, or maybe you just want to ask if God has anything to say to you. Listen. Write down whatever comes to mind:

You can make sure it is truly God speaking with this quick test:

1. Does it line up with the teachings of the Bible?

2. Does it glorify God, and advance His Kingdom (rather than my own agenda)?

As you listen and evaluate what you hear with the Scripture: receive whatever you hear God saying. And when applicable, commit to obey it. Make this a regular practice in your life!

Begin praying specifically, seeking God and His Word for ways that He might be leading you to bring specific requests to Him. In your journal, draw a vertical line down the center of the page—on the left side write "prayer requests" and on the right side write "answers."

Regularly write down your requests on the left along with the date. Continue to go back and pray for those things, writing down the answer in the right column when you witness God resolve your request. Consider using the prayer journal in *Up-Close: A Spiritual Life Notebook* for this.

Additionally, continue to pray specifically for ALL the people in your life who do not know Jesus yet—both people you continue to meet and your list in Chapter 2.

BEGIN MEMORIZING THE MEMORY VERSE:

——————————————————————————————

"Don't worry about anything, but in everything, through prayer and petition with thanksgiving, let your requests be made known to God." — Philippians 4:6, CSB

——————————————————————————————

BONUS Verse: "And the peace of God, which surpasses all understanding, will guard your hearts and minds in Christ Jesus." — Philippians 4:7, CSB

——————————————————————————————

WHAT IF . . . ?

Last week you were challenged to share Scripture with someone else to encourage them in their faith journey (a word of encouragement, or a text, a letter, an email etc.). This week, pray specifically for them. Pray for specific hopes and dreams that God may place on your heart for them. Now, reach out to them again, letting them know you have prayed for them. Share any specific hopes or dreams you have brought to God in prayer for their life. And if you have any Scripture you would like to share, send that too!

DISCUSSION

1. Share any victories or obstacles from last week's action steps.
2. Pray together.
3. Review Memory Verse.
4. Read Key Scriptures: 1 Thessalonians 5:17; Philippians 4:6-7; Matthew 6:9-13.
5. Review key concepts from the chapter. Share how you are processing and any comments you have. Did anything in

particular really resonate with you? Is there anything you disagreed with? Or is there anything you will never forget? Do you have any questions about it?

6. Where do you need to grow most in prayer—in one of the categories of P.R.A.Y. (Praise, Repent, Ask, Yield)? In listening for His voice and being led by the Holy Spirit? In praying specifically? In praying constantly? How will you begin to grow in prayer this week?

7. What do you believe God was speaking to you as you prayed this week in the "Now What" section?

8. What things did you write down in the "Now What" section that you feel led to begin praying specifically for?

9. Review "What If . . . " Section and the Memory Verse again.

10. Everyone share—what is your one key takeaway or action step for this week?

11. Pray together.

OTHER HELPFUL RESOURCES:

Up-Close: A Spiritual Life Notebook to Fuel Your Growth in Christ by Forge (Look for the "Prayer Requests" Section).

Ten-Finger Prayers (Book) by Agnes Robertson

For purchasing options and more resources, go to:
MultiplyMore.com

NOTES
Pursuing Passionate Prayer

NOTES
Pursuing Passionate Prayer

6

PARTICIPATING IN THE LOCAL CHURCH

Acts 2:42 • 1 Corinthians 14:26 • Ephesians 4:12

**The Church is a gathering of God's people,
built on the truth of who Jesus is.**

This is the first time in Scripture we see the word "_____."
(Matthew 16:18)

The Church will be built on the truth who Jesus is, the Christ, the
_____. (1 Peter 2:6)

The Church is a _____ of God's people.

Jesus said, "I will build _____ Church"

Jesus is claiming ownership of the Church. It is His responsibility to build a church and to shut one down.

Many have tried to stomp out the Church for over 2,000 years, but they have not succeeded.

If You Are a Christian, You Go to Church

- We need the church for our _____.

- We need the church to worship with other believers.

- We need the church to be equipped to scatter for ministry.

- We need the church to help resolve our conflict with other believers. (Matthew 18:15-20)

Believers Gather for... (Acts 2:42)

_____ – God's Word.

_____ – Relationship with other believers; we are not meant to live in isolation.

_____ ___ _____ – Communion, commemorating the death and resurrection of Jesus.

_____ – Communicating with God together, praying with and for one another; and bringing your tithe/giving as offering and prayerful worship to God.

God has given various giftings in the church to equip every ordinary believer to do the work of the ministry. (Ephesians 4:12)

We gather for worship and then _____ for ministry.

The church is not a building or a location, but a local _____ of believers who come together as God has commanded. (Hebrews 10:25)

NOW WHAT?

Are you involved in a local church? Why or why not?

Jesus is calling you to get involved and engage the local church. If you are not already engaged in a local church, you need to find a church.

FINDING A CHURCH

What to look for in finding a church:

- Focused on Jesus above all else (Hebrews 12:2).
- Actively engaging God's Word (the Bible) to equip every believer (Ephesians 4:12).
- Focused on engaging God's mission/the Great Commission (Matthew 28:18-20).
- Includes the practices of Acts 2:42—teaching from God's Word, fellowship, breaking of bread, and prayer.
- Consider looking for options using the Billy Graham Evangelistic Association's church locator tool: Churches.GoingFarther.net.

Starting a Church

Maybe there are no churches in your area, and God is leading you to start one. Take a look at Appendix B for additional tips on launching a church gathering.

Have you criticized the Bride of Christ instead of building her up? How so?

Pray and ask for God's forgiveness if you have been critical out of a complaining heart. Rather than complaining and criticizing from the outside, how can you begin to serve and be a part of the solution to the potential problems you see?

What are your spiritual gifts?

Read through the spiritual gifts listed in Romans 12:6-8; 1 Corinthians 12:7-11, 28; and Exodus 31:3-5.

This week, take the **spiritual gifts assessment here: ForgeForward.org/Spiritual-Gifts-Test**

After prayerfully studying these Scriptures and taking the spiritual gifts assessment, list your spiritual gifts here:

After completing the above, ask God how He has created you to serve His Kingdom and prayerfully brainstorm how you can use your gifts to serve your local church. As you pray, write down your ideas here:

After prayerfully brainstorming, consider meeting with the appropriate leaders or mentors in your church setting and ask how you can use your gifts to serve and be a blessing.

BEGIN MEMORIZING THE MEMORY VERSE:

"... Let us not neglect our meeting together, as some people do, but encourage each other ..." — Hebrews 10:25a, ESV

WHAT IF ... ?

As you engage in your local church, remember, God has not called you to be a mere spectator, but to be a participant. So, look around. Are there people who have not yet had an opportunity to be spiritually invested in and encouraged and are waiting for someone to do so? Are there lives God wants you to come alongside so that they too could discover how to engage far beyond sitting and listening in a once-a-week gathering, ultimately learning to live out a 24/7 life of vibrantly seeking God and living for His purposes? Remember, this does not require a title or a position. God desires His entire body to be actively engaged, living out His resurrected life!

What if you joined God in coming alongside others who are still waiting for an opportunity to receive everything *Multiplying Movements* provides? This tool is meant for you, but not only for you! God desires to multiply your impact through others. There are still people in all sorts of "harvest fields" waiting for Kingdom Laborers to bring Jesus up-close, and *you* could be the answer to seeing God's movement begin to expand!

You have been considering and praying over various people the last several weeks, and even encouraging some too. They are likely people God wants you to consider coming alongside using *Multiplying Movements* (after you finish it). It is time to prayerfully decide, "Who will I invite to go through Multiplying Movements with me?" It could be one person or several. Never underestimate just one life!

As of now, you likely don't feel ready for this. That is okay. Now is simply the time to begin praying for others that God will place (or already has placed) in your path! As you consider who they might be, write their name (or names) here, and then begin praying for them daily this week:

DISCUSSION

1. Share any victories or obstacles from last week's action steps.
2. Pray together.
3. Review Memory Verse.
4. Read Key Scriptures: Acts 2:42; 1 Corinthians 14:26; Ephesians 4:12.
5. Review key concepts from the chapter. Share how you are processing and any comments you have. Did anything in particular really resonate with you? Is there anything you disagreed with? Or is there anything you will never forget? Do you have any questions about it?
6. Describe what your current local church involvement looks like.
7. What do you believe are your spiritual gifts?
8. Do you see any potential shortcomings in your church? Do you believe God revealed anything to you in prayer this week about your gifts? What surfaced in your brainstorming? Based on these factors, how can you serve your church / other believers with your gifts going forward?
9. Review "What If . . ." Section and the Memory Verse again.
10. Everyone share—what is your one key takeaway or action step for this week?
11. Pray together.

OTHER HELPFUL RESOURCES:

Now What? Practical Tips to Fuel Your Faith (booklet) "Chapter 5: Hanging Out with Other Christians," by Forge

For purchasing options and more resources, go to:
MultiplyMore.com

NOTES
Participating in the Local Church

7

REDISCOVERING THE GOOD NEWS

1 Corinthians 15:1, 3-4 • 1 Peter 3:18 • Mark 1:14-15

**What does the Scripture say
is most important?**

The _____ is of first importance. So, what exactly is it?

"Gospel" means _____ _____.

"Good news" was used to announce kings in great military victories in ancient times. In the Gospel, Jesus is announced as the new King!

So, how did Jesus unveil His kingship?...

Christ died for our sins.

We are born _____ from God because of our sin.
(Isaiah 59:2)

Sin leads to _____. (Romans 3:23)

No one can cross the gap to God. The sin chasm is too wide.

Therefore, _____ comes to us, paying the price for
our sin!

Jesus took our place and our penalty for our sin, to bring us to
God. (1 Peter 3:18)

Christ was buried.

Jesus could not have survived Roman flogging and crucifixion.
The Romans were expert executioners.

Jesus really was _____. He truly did take on the
punishment for our sin.

Three days later Christ raised from the dead.

Jesus really did rise from the dead, not just spiritually but
physically.

Jesus' resurrection is the most important moment in history!

Jesus' _____ is the "lynchpin" of Christianity. Without it, everything falls apart. Without the _____, we don't have Christianity. (1 Corinthians 15:14)

With the resurrection, we have the most amazing news ever told!

If Jesus really did rise from the dead:

- All of our _____ is worthwhile.

- Our faith is founded on the Rock, who is Jesus.

- The death of Jesus really did pay the price for our _____.

- We will be resurrected too when Jesus returns.

- We can be filled with joy, peace, and contentment.

Jesus appeared to many people, proving His resurrection and power to transform lives! (1 Corinthians 15:5-8)

The Good News!

Jesus died for our sin, was buried, and rose from the dead, revealing that He really is the one true King and Lord of all.

The Good News should affect _____ aspect of our lives:

- We must know it, understand it, and share it.

- Our relationships should reflect the Good News of Jesus and His love. (Ephesians 5-6)

- Embracing the Good News impacts how we invest our money for the Kingdom.

- The Good News should impact the choices we make.

- The Good News is for every day of the week, for every moment.

NOW WHAT?

Before this teaching, how would you have described the "Gospel" or the "Good News"? Did it shift at all based on this message? How so?

What aspect of the Good News do you need to spend more time digging into? How can you engage that aspect more fully?

Has the Good News fully impacted every part of your life? Where do you need to allow God to more fully impact you—any key relationships? Your finances? Your choices in this season of life? How you invest your time?

BEGIN MEMORIZING THE MEMORY VERSE:

— —

"... I want to remind you of the Gospel ... For I passed on to you as most important what I also received: that *Christ died for our sins* according to the Scriptures, that He was buried, that *He was raised on the third day* according to the Scriptures." — 1 Corinthians 15:3-4, CSB, emphasis mine

— —

WHAT IF ... ?

The Good News impacts all of our relationships! We are blessed to be a blessing (Genesis 12:2). What Jesus did is for us, but not only for us. As the memory verse declares, it is meant to be "passed!" We cannot afford to take the *it's-all-about-me,* selfish stance in our actions, only receiving and never giving. Jesus died for the entire world (1 John 2:2) and longs to have people not only accepting salvation, but also following Him into a life of everyday commitment and impact (Matthew 4:19)!

And—just as Jesus Himself modeled and called every one of His followers to live out—it most often requires coming alongside others to help them discover not only salvation but also the full implications of the Good News, allowing the light of Jesus to permeate every aspect of their lives and relationships.

So, go ahead and write out a brief paragraph of what Jesus has been doing in your life through *Multiplying Movements*, so that you can send it over to those you have been encouraging and praying for over the last several weeks, sharing the impact of what you have received:

When you send it, include a message like this:

"I hope to invite some others to go through this same 12-week opportunity with me, to talk about God's plan for our lives and grow spiritually as we go through a resource called *Multiplying Movements*! I am planning to start about 6 weeks from now. Would you be interested in joining me?"

Take a few minutes now to send this to the people you wrote down last week and any others that God has been putting on your heart. You could also share this in conversation with those God brings to you this week or even post it on social media if you want to. Then you will begin to see who God has for you to come alongside using *Multiplying Movements*.

DISCUSSION

1. Share any victories or obstacles from last week's action steps.
2. Pray together.
3. Review Memory Verse.
4. Read Key Scriptures: 1 Corinthians 15:1-4; 1 Peter 3:18; Mark 1:14-15.
5. Review key concepts from the chapter. Share how you are processing and any comments you have. Did anything in particular really resonate with you? Is there anything you disagreed with? Or is there anything you will never forget? Do you have any questions about it?
6. Before this message, did you fully understand the Gospel and its implications for all of life? Did any portion bring a renewed perspective for you? How so?
7. What part of your life do you need to allow the Good News of Jesus to more fully impact?
8. Review "What If . . ." Section and the Memory Verse again.
9. Everyone share—what is your one key takeaway or action step for this week?
10. Pray together.

OTHER HELPFUL RESOURCES:

Now What?: Practical Tips to Fuel Your Faith (Booklet) by Forge

For purchasing options and more resources, go to:
MultiplyMore.com

NOTES
Rediscovering the Good News

OVERCOMING HINDRANCES

Hebrews 12:1-2 • Galatians 5:1 • Hebrews 4:16

Throwing off everything that hinders to run our unique races of loving God, loving others, and advancing His Kingdom!

It is like we are running a race with chains holding us back...

WHAT "CHAINS" MIGHT BE HINDERING US?

_____ **Sin** (1 John 1:9)

- Our sin is often rooted in pride, evil desires, and division.

- Rather than confess our sin we often choose to live in darkness.

. . .

_____ **Lies** (John 8:32)

- When we don't know the _____, we begin to believe lies.

- When we are not engaging the _____, we begin to believe lies.

_____ (Colossians 3:13)

- We are to forgive those who wrong us in the same way that God has forgiven us in Christ.

- When we don't forgive, it is like a wound that begins to fester with disease and becomes worse. Our healing begins with

  _____.

_____ **Relationships** (1 Corinthians 15:33)

- Anyone in your life having a stronger influence in your life than God Himself...

- Children dishonoring and disobeying your parents, wives not submitting to your husbands, husbands disrespecting and not loving your wives in the same way Jesus did the Church, physical intimacy outside of marriage.

_____ **Patterns** (1 Peter 1:18)

- An empty way of life, sin, and negativity passed down to you from your family.

- Jesus has set us free from this but we often walk in old ways rather than in the newness of life.

Spiritual _____ (James 4:7)

- Satan is seeking to attack believers (Ephesians 6:16; 1 Peter 5:8), especially those who are obeying Jesus and laboring for His Kingdom. (Revelation 12:9, 17)

- When we don't submit to God and resist the enemy's attacks, the devil may gain a place of influence (a foothold) in our lives. (Ephesians 4:26)

5 Weapons of our Warfare:

1. Scripture out loud. (Memorize Scripture!)

2. The name of Jesus out loud.

3. The armor of God. (Ephesians 6:10-17)

4. Prayer.

5. Praise.

HOW DO WE THROW OFF EVERYTHING THAT HINDERS?

Above all, look to _____! Then begin to do what His Word teaches us:

- Confess your sin.

- Rebuke lies and receive God's truth.

- Forgive those who have wronged you.

- Rebuke negative generational patterns and embrace God's plan for your future.

- Leave behind unhealthy relationships and seek godly ones.

- Rebuke the enemy's attack in your life: "In Jesus' name go away!"

It is for freedom that Jesus has set you free; do not be
_____ all over again! (Galatians 5:1)

———————

Will you choose the chains
or the freedom
that Jesus has purchased for you?

———————

NOW WHAT?

Spend some time now and ask Jesus, "What are the chains hindering my life right now?" Write them here:

Continue in prayer, dealing with each chain that you have recognized is in your life. Do what God's Word teaches us to do with each one of these hindrances.

Dealing with our chains is not a "one and done" event. Most often, even after chains are removed, we still have to be intentional to change our patterns and habits. We must continue throwing off *everything* **that hinders throughout all of life. From this day forward, as hindering chains come up, deal with them immediately in prayer!**

BEGIN MEMORIZING THE MEMORY VERSE:

—————————————————————

"... Let us lay aside every weight, and the sin that so easily ensnares us, and let us run with endurance the race that is set before us." — Hebrews 12:1b, NKJV

—————————————————————

WHAT IF . . . ?

As you consider stepping out to come alongside other lives using *Multiplying Movements*, do not let the enemy's lies and accusations hold you back from inviting others into the journey! The enemy of your soul may begin to send lies attempting to increase insecurity, crippling your impact.

Do not let pride overtake you, nor let fear have the final say. Do not believe any thought that declares *God cannot use me due to what I have done or where I have been*, or *I do not have what it takes* or *what if I don't do this well enough?*

Rebuke those lies in the name of Jesus and receive the truth that He is more than able to empower you (Ephesians 3:16)! You must determine that Jesus will be your leader so that you won't be led by fear or anything else.

Now, go back to your list of friends in the recent "What If . . . ? Sections. Reach out to them again this week.

If you haven't heard back from them, send a message like this:

"Hi [NAME], Did you have any further thoughts on joining me? I would be really excited if you did!

We're planning to meet once a week over the next few months to really go deep and dive into the Bible together. We'll be using a resource called *Multiplying Movements*. As I had mentioned in my last message, God has been using it to change my life and teach me so much, and I can't wait to share it with you!

Let me know what you think."

If you have heard back from them and they plan to join, then go ahead and send them a message like this:

"I am really excited to do this with you! We're planning to meet once a week over the next few months to really go deep and dive into the

Bible together. As I had mentioned in my last message, God has been using *Multiplying Movements* to change my life and teach me so much, and I can't wait to share it with you! I will be in touch soon with some weekly day / time options."

Some may say "yes" to your invitation and some may say "no." But, be encouraged, that a present "no" from someone you invite, does not always mean a long-term, definite "no." You may invite them again later and they say "yes" in a different season of life. And a current "no" also frees you up to spend even more time presently with someone else that God may want you to come alongside.

DISCUSSION

1. Share any victories or obstacles from last week's action steps.
2. Pray together.
3. Review Memory Verse.
4. Read Key Scriptures: Hebrews 12:1-2; Galatians 5:1; Hebrews 4:16.
5. Review key concepts from the chapter. Share how you are processing and any comments you have. Did anything in particular really resonate with you? Is there anything you disagreed with? Or is there anything you will never forget? Do you have any questions about it?
6. What chains or hindrances did God reveal in your life? Were you able to deal with them in prayer this week? If so, how did it go? If not, what is holding you back?
7. For the following questions, after someone shares, encourage with God's truth and go to Jesus together, praying through whatever surfaces:
   a. Are there any other areas of your heart or life that still feel blocked or closed off from the fullness of freedom Jesus has for you?
   b. Is there any sin in your life that you feel you need to confess to God with each other to fully walk in freedom?

8. Consider this crucial reality as you step forward, continuing to walk in Christ's freedom: Culture can even hinder you, pulling you in and deceiving you with lies. What does your current relationship with the world's culture look like? Are you consuming more of culture than you are God's Word and truth? Are there any shifts you need to make (Romans 12:2)?

9. Review "What If . . ." Section and the Memory Verse again.

10. Everyone share—what is your one key takeaway or action step for this week?

11. Pray together.

OTHER HELPFUL RESOURCES:

"Spiritual Warfare" sermon and book by Charlie Marq: ForgeForward.org/war

This message will help you dig deeper into the topic, including helpful ways to pray through spiritual warfare in your life.

For this resource and many more, go to: **MultiplyMore.com**

NOTES
Overcoming Hindrances

----

(9)

WALKING BY FAITH

Hebrews 11:1-12, 17-38 • Matthew 4:19-20 • Matthew 14:27-31

**Joining Jesus on a Kingdom-advancing adventure,
full of meaning and purpose!**

The Journey of Living by Faith...

FOUNDATIONAL FAITH

Whoever receives Him, becomes a child of God.

Your relationship with God began with you responding to His initiative.

At this stage, you begin establishing an understanding of His ways and your inheritance in Christ.

God is _____ you up and deepening your roots. (Colossians 2:6-7)

Yet, Jesus invites us beyond foundational faith into an adventure full of meaning and purpose… Jesus doesn't want us to just be well-taught but well-_____.

```
┌─────────────────┐
│   A CALL         │
│   TO FAITH       │
└─────────────────┘
```

THE CALL

What does this call to adventure and impact, to faith-walking look like? How do you know it's God?

- There will most often be a _____ of God's prompting.

- It will often be confirmed through _____.

- It will often be affirmed by objective, godly others.

A life of faith is not about how much information we can pack into our brains, not about how well-taught we are, but how well-walked we will be. It's about taking action and joining the adventure.

THE INTERNAL BATTLE

As God asks you to step out and step forward, fear and obstacles will come at you, trying to pull you back.

At times, people around you will even ask you how this will really work out?

- Your response: "___ _____ _____. I may not have the answer, but I do have assurance that this is what I am supposed to do, and I know that God must know. It is my role to trust Him."

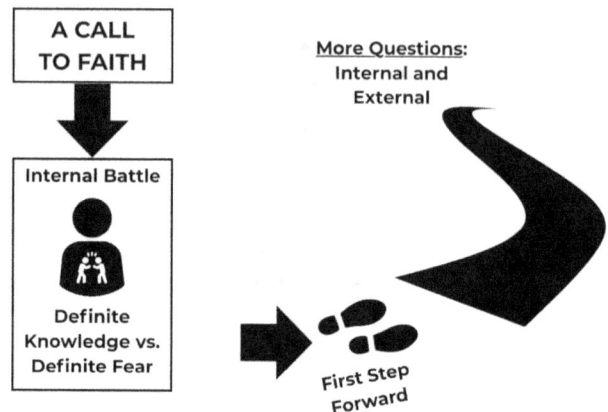

THE FIRST STEP FORWARD

Don't think you know how to do this. Let _____ direct your steps and the entire journey. Let Him show you how—all along the way.

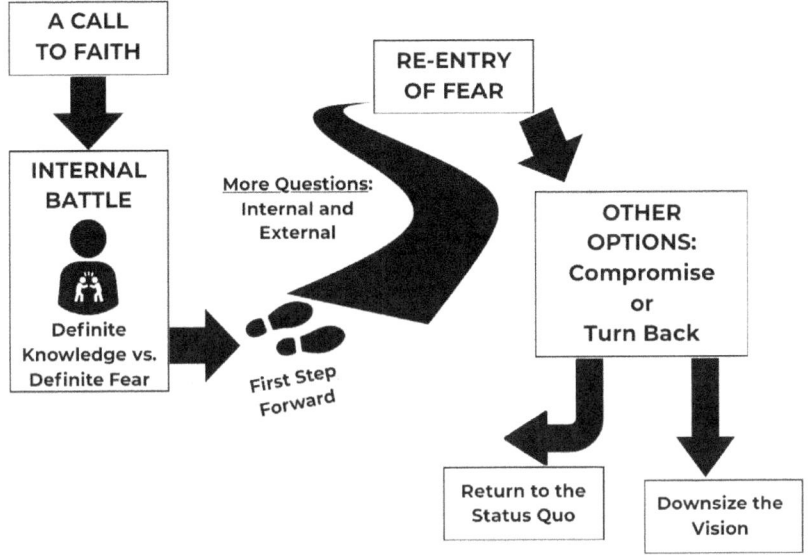

THE RE-ENTRY OF FEAR

- Fear _____ and doubts.

- Fear needs every _____ in place, but that's not possible because you are walking by faith.

- Fear requires a high false security.

Practice Proverbs 3:5-6, as you walk forward in what God is calling you to do!

Fear cannot be your _____!

If you allow fear to be your leader, it will tell you to:

- Compromise and down-size the vision.

- Turn and run.

At this point in the faith journey, often out of necessity, you will go deeper with God.

Do not look logically at what can happen.

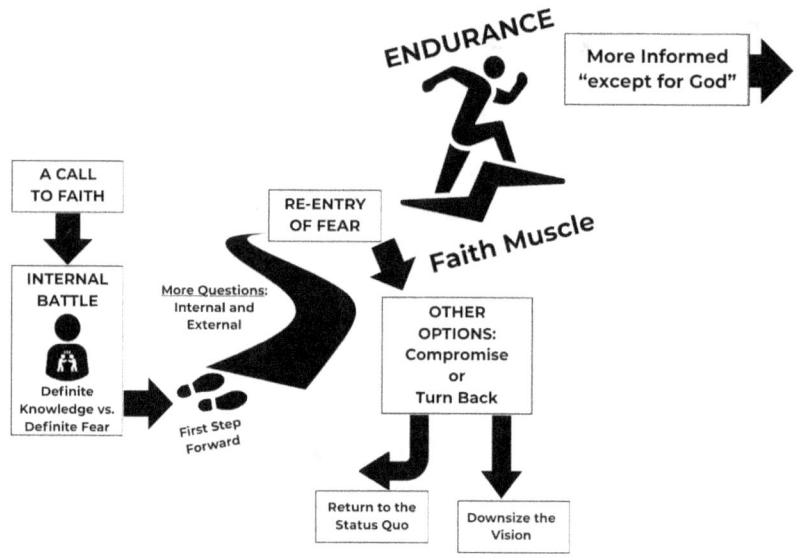

ENDURANCE

Fix your eyes on _____, who endured (Hebrews 12:3), so that you can endure!

- Remember who your _____ is.

- Focus on who your God has been for others in history.

- Remember the _____, and hold onto God's promises.

- Remember your earlier days (when you faced a challenge and witnessed God come through).

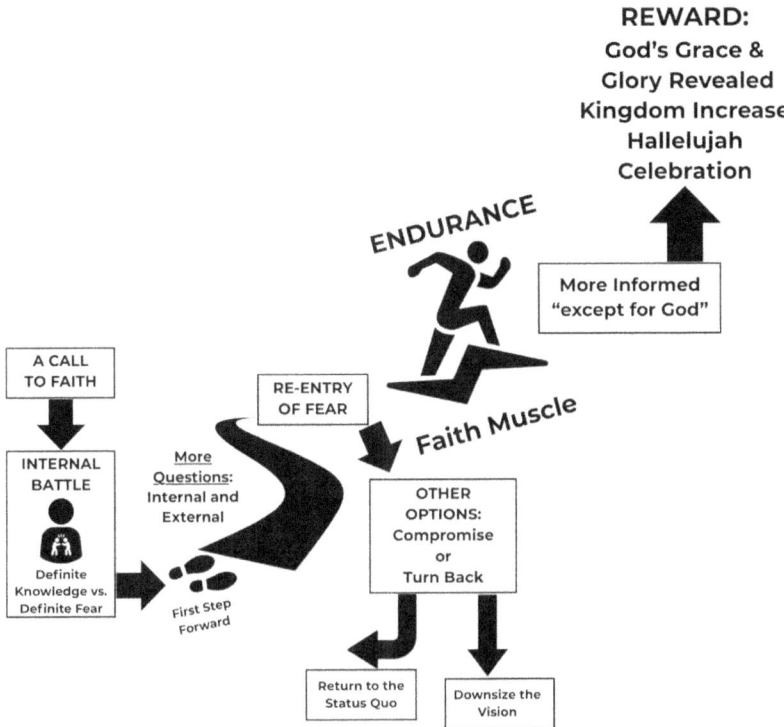

THE REWARD OF WALKING BY FAITH

- God's grace and glory revealed.

- Kingdom increase.

- Hallelujah celebration!

"_____ _____, good and faithful servant."

NOW WHAT?

Spend some time in prayer right now asking God, "How do you want me to step out in faith, joining you in a Kingdom adventure?" Write down anything that comes to mind—whatever God burdens your heart with or whatever dreams for the world He brings, no matter how big or impossible they may be:

When you think about what God might be calling you to do, what fears arise? Write them down and give them over to God in prayer:

Continue to look for God's reoccurring prompting (whether in the Word, in prayer, through others, etc.). As they come, write down and journal any potential confirmations or leadings, so that you do not forget, and so that your faith and confidence in Him are built up!

What is one way that you can take a step of faith this week?

BEGIN MEMORIZING THE MEMORY VERSE:

————————————————————————

"Trust in the LORD with all your heart; and do not rely on your own understanding; in all your ways know Him, and He will make your paths straight" — Proverbs 3:5-6, CSB

————————————————————————

WHAT IF . . . ?

You have taken your first steps to come alongside other lives! Great job! Yes, you may be nervous and don't know fully what to expect. As you step out, nervousness is normal. But you must not let fear be your leader. Fear will try to stop you from engaging any one life God puts in front of you! If you let fear have the final say, it will cripple you from the joy of seeing God ignite and empower other lives through you!

Rather, decide to walk by faith trusting that God will provide what you need and bring wisdom for what you don't know—whether in a moment or over time.

As you choose to venture out in faith coming alongside others, you will be amazed by all God does, spurring on a movement of Kingdom Laborers through you! Keep praying for those you have invited and keep asking God to bring you anyone else that He wants you to come alongside.

Take a look at your weekly schedule and select several options on different days for a 75-minute Multiplying Movements meeting time. Eventually you will narrow it down to have a consistent weekly meeting rhythm for you and the person or people that you will come alongside.

Right now, it's time to reach out again:

For any new person God puts on your heart, use the same message you sent out over the last two weeks from Chapters 7-8.

For those you have not yet heard an answer from, reach out and simply ask:

"Do you have any further thoughts on joining me when we begin getting together? I am praying for you!"

For those who have shared that they plan to join you, send a message along these lines:

"I am praying for all God will do when we meet together! Will you let me know if any of the following days / times will work for you once we start?

[INSERT DAY / TIME OPTIONS - Consider using a meeting survey tool like Doodle.com if you are inviting more than 1-2 people and need help choosing a time that works for everyone]."

DISCUSSION

1. Share any victories or obstacles from last week's action steps.
2. Pray together.

3. Review Memory Verse.

4. Read Key Scriptures: Matthew 4:19-20; Matthew 14:27-31.

5. Review key concepts from the chapter. Share how you are processing and any comments you have. Did anything in particular really resonate with you? Is there anything you disagreed with? Or is there anything you will never forget? Do you have any questions about it?

6. How is God calling you to step out in faith in this season of your life?

7. What fears or obstacles rise up as you consider stepping out in faith? Or in what aspect of your life are you afraid to live by faith?

8. As you think about coming alongside others using *Multiplying Movements*, where do you land on the faith diagram from the chapter? How would you describe your inner feelings, apprehensions, thoughts, or commitment level to stepping out in faith in response to Jesus' command to "make disciples" by spiritually investing in others?

9. Realizing that you spell faith "R-I-S-K," and that stepping out for Jesus is always a worthy risk—how will you begin to step out in faith this week?

10. Review "What If . . . " Section and the Memory Verse again.

11. Everyone share—what is your one key takeaway or action step for this week?

12. Read Hebrews 11 together as an encouragement—*breathing courage into you*—for your initial steps of faith this week!

13. Pray together.

OTHER HELPFUL RESOURCES:

It's My Turn: 20 Kingdom Laborers Who Changed Their World and Compel Me to Impact Mine (Book) by Forge

For purchasing options and more resources, go to:
MultiplyMore.com

NOTES
Walking by Faith

_____

_____

_____

_____

_____

_____

_____

_____

_____

_____

_____

_____

_____

NOTES
Walking by Faith

10

UTILIZING YOUR UNIQUE MINISTRY

1 Corinthians 12:5 • 1 Corinthians 12:18 • Ephesians 2:10

**Meeting people at their point of need,
using the uniqueness of our lives.**

WHAT IS MINISTRY?

_____ is meeting people at their point of need.

Ministry happens in real life, in real space, with real people, and is meeting real needs.

Each one of us should use whatever gift we have received to _____ others. (1 Peter 4:10)

Outside of church gatherings, there are _____ plus hours in the week to live out ministry as unique as you are.

Just like David did not fit in Saul's armor, each of us do not fit perfect "ministry" molds.

- Each of us have unique God-given _____.
- God has designed you with a ministry purpose in mind.

HOW TO DISCOVER YOUR UNIQUE ABILITIES AND MINISTRY PURPOSE:

1. Ask God, your creator-designer.

2. Get into the _____ and allow God to show you His plan.

You will see and notice things others don't see. Ministry can look like you!

GOD DESIRES TO EMPLOY YOUR _____ LIFE FOR HIS MINISTRY PURPOSES:

- Using your uniqueness, you will reach people no one else can? No pastor nor missionary is positioned to reach the people God is asking *you* to reach!

- God can employ your _____ and your spiritual gifts.

- God can employ your _____ and interests.

- God can employ your God-story.

- God can employ the _____ you go: where you work, where you live, where you have fun, wherever you go daily.

- God can employ your _____ _____.

- God can employ your tragedy, pain, and suffering.

NOW WHAT?

Spend some time praying right now. Ask God to help you see unique ministry opportunities He has created you for.

What Does Ministry Look Like?

Often, we tend to believe that to be in ministry, we must be a pastor, missionary, musician, or some other "typical" ministry vocation. But that is just not the case. God has created each of us uniquely to carry out the distinct ministry He has called us to. We can use our gifts, passions, hobbies, and interests for the Kingdom. What is unique about you that can be used for the Kingdom?

Do a quick inventory of the things in your life that God can employ to impact the world.

One of the greatest joys in life comes when we live out God's purpose for us. He has designed each of us like no other and His design is perfect for Kingdom impact. Perhaps that is why God seems to give us the entrepreneurial freedom to creatively apply our gifts and passions to advance His Kingdom.

What could everyday impact look like if it is as distinct and unique as you are? We invite you to do an inventory of the things in your life that God can employ. It could help you discover more about how God can employ who you are to minister to others where they are.

PERSONAL MINISTRY INVENTORY

What are your hobbies and/or recreational interests?

☐ Fly Fishing

☐ Cooking/Baking

☐ Running/Working Out

☐ Skateboarding

▫ Gardening or Lawn Work

▫ Investing

▫ Traveling

▫ Motorcycling/Bicycling

▫ Knitting/Sewing

▫ Painting

▫ _____

▫ _____

What season of life are you in?

▫ Student

▫ Single

▫ Professional

▫ Early Married

▫ Parents of Young Children

▫ Parents of Teenagers

▫ Empty Nester

▫ Retired

▫ _____

▫ _____

What financial/physical resources do you have to offer?

▫ Guest Room or property

▫ Transportation/Extra Vehicle /Ability to Drive Others

▫ Camping or Adventure Gear

▫ Reward Points/Frequent Flyer Miles

▫ Tools and Equipment/A Lawn Mower

▫ Legacy Giving

▫ Stock Giving

▫ Savings & Investments

▫ _____

▫ _____

What are some life experiences you have had?

▫ Travel Experiences

▫ Job Experiences

▫ Relationship Experiences

▫ Educational Experiences

▫ _____

▫ _____

What are some painful life experiences you have had (past or current)?

▫ Cancer Survivor

▫ Loss of a Child or Other Family Member

▫ Injury

▫ Spiritual Struggle

▢ Dark-Night of the Soul (a season of pain, struggle, or spiritual wrestling)

▢ Loneliness

▢ _____

▢ _____

Do you have any special skills?

▢ Mechanical

▢ Hospitality

▢ Art/Photography/Videography

▢ Music

▢ Carpentry

▢ Writing

▢ Caregiving

▢ Sports

▢ Education

▢ Outdoor/Survival Skills

▢ Communication

▢ Organization

▢ _____

▢ _____

WHERE AND WHEN DOES MINISTRY HAPPEN?

Think about it for a second . . . ministry happens in the ordinary venues of life. Not only at church, a Christian conference, retreat, or on a short-term mission trip.

Here are some examples:

- □ With our families

- □ At our church

- □ At work

- □ In our neighborhoods

- □ At events

- □ At block parties

- □ With our neighbors and their interests

- □ At school

- □ In a dorm

- □ At our lockers

- □ In our classes

- □ At the student union

- □ In our communities

- □ In our clubs

- □ In our civic organizations

- □ At parent-teacher organizations

- □ With our boards

▫ At rescue missions

▫ At ministry organizations

▫ Along the way

▫ In the grocery store

▫ At a restaurant

▫ At the bank

▫ At the gas station

▫ At the post office

Where are the ordinary venues in *your* life?

Next Steps

Now that you have begun to identify what ministry can look like (your unique hobbies, interests and passions) and you know where and when ministry can take place (the ordinary venues in your life), here are some next steps to help you carry out your unique and distinct ministry.

• Look back at your inventory and see how your unique hobbies, interests and passions can be specifically applied to ministry in your life situations.

- Prayerfully ask God to give you opportunities for ministry.
- Take time to search the Scriptures for verses about your giftings. Take note how others in the Scriptures used similar gift-sets to glorify God and reach others.
- Read a book about your area of unique ministry.
- Talk to a trusted Christian friend, parent, mentor, or spiritual leader about your unique, everyday ministry ideas. Brainstorm how you can use your uniqueness to glorify God and minister to others.
- Make a list of the people and places that could benefit from your ministry.

What will you do this week to begin connecting with others using your unique ministry?

BEGIN MEMORIZING THE MEMORY VERSE:

————————————————————————

"Each of you should use whatever gift you have received to serve others . . . " 1 Peter 4:10, NIV

————————————————————————

WHAT IF . . . ?

Remember, ministry is simply meeting people at their point of need. And most people have been over-entertained, under-challenged, and ill-equipped to live the life God intends for them. That's where you come in! Your uniqueness may be the very reason that you have a relationship with people that no missionary or pastor ever has. You are uniquely positioned to have the respect and relational camaraderie with the people God is placing in your life, and therefore will be able to uniquely help them discover the life God has for them!

Perhaps you want to prayerfully consider utilizing your uniqueness to strengthen your *Multiplying Movements* relationships through shared recreational activities, hobbies, interests, or restaurant tastes. After your *Multiplying Movements* meeting times, you all could go do something together, and even invite lost people that you all have been praying for!

Take a few moments now to pray for the friends who will be joining you in the weeks ahead. Ask God to help you empower them to discover *their* unique impact.

Right now, it would be helpful to follow-up with everyone who has agreed to meet together, sending them a message along the lines of the following:

"Hi [NAME]! We will plan to meet each week on [DAY at TIME] [at

LOCATION OR BY VIDEO] for about 75 minutes of discussion and prayer. Our time should go for about 12-14 weeks.

Before each time we meet, we will each read the *Multiplying Movements* chapter (or watch the video) and personally process through the "Now What" and "What If?" reflection sections.

To be ready to meet in about three weeks, will you go ahead and order either the book or video workbook at **MultiplyingMovements.com**?

I am very excited to start meeting and see all God has for us!"

DISCUSSION

1. Share any victories or obstacles from last week's action steps.
2. Pray together.
3. Review Memory Verse.
4. Read Key Scriptures: 1 Corinthians 12:5; 1 Corinthians 12:18; Ephesians 2:10.
5. Review key concepts from the chapter. Share how you are processing and any comments you have. Did anything in particular really resonate with you? Is there anything you disagreed with? Or is there anything you will never forget? Do you have any questions about it?
6. What portions of your life have you never considered being "employable" by God?
7. What did you discover as you went through the Personal Ministry Inventory? Did anything surprise you?
8. If you began to approach each of area of your life with intentionality, as employable for God's Kingdom, what might begin happening?
9. This week, how will you begin utilizing your uniqueness to build bridges to others as you see, stop, and spend time with them?
10. Review "What If . . . " Section and the Memory Verse again.

11. Everyone share—what is your one key takeaway or action step for this week?

12. Pray together.

OTHER HELPFUL RESOURCES:

Plan A: Discovering Your Everyday, Everywhere Unique Purpose (book and audio) by Dwight Robertson

For purchasing options and more resources, go to:

MultiplyMore.com

NOTES

Utilizing Your Unique Ministry

NOTES

Utilizing Your Unique Ministry

ENGAGING LOST PEOPLE

Colossians 1:26-27 • Mark 5:18-20 • Acts 8:4

**We need to tell as many people
as we can about Christ!**

Adam and Eve before the fall: _____, without sin.

Adam BEFORE the Fall

GOD

Adam and Eve after the fall: Sinful.

Adam AFTER the Fall

Sin has dominion over them (arrows up). This is the reality for all of humanity after them.

Those who believe in Jesus: Victorious.

NORMAL CHRISTIAN

Sin no longer has dominion. It is still present, but it has been crucified (arrows down).

What is in the circle?! …

God goes to _____ _____ to bring the lost to
Himself!

Extreme Measure #1 – _____ from Heaven. (1 Kings 18)

Extreme Measure #2 – _____. (Jonah)

Extreme Measure #3 – _____ (fell to the ground and grew the
tree that became the cross of Christ).

… There are a lot of extreme measures throughout the Scriptures.

Final Extreme Measure…

_____ in you. (Colossians 1:26-27)

The _____ _____ in you. (Ephesians 1:13-14)

The _____ in you. (John 14:23)

The Father, Son, and Holy Spirit are all three _____ you!

_____ **are the extreme measure of God!**

You are the most powerful entity on this planet.
That's why we need to tell as many as we can about _____!

WHAT DOES IT LOOK LIKE TO TELL OTHERS ABOUT JESUS?

A very practical and powerful way to tell others about Jesus is to share our stories of what He has done in our lives. What would that look like?

- Share what your life was like before encountering Jesus. What difficulty did you face? What negative things did you experience? What misconceptions did you have about God?

- Share how you encountered Jesus—what did that time look like, and what led to it (prayer time, someone told you, etc.)?

- Share about how Jesus changed your life. What is now different in your life because of Jesus? What is the real change Jesus has brought? Maybe you are wondering, "What if I believed in Jesus when I was really young and don't have a before/after story?" Your story might be your salvation experience, but it might also be a post-salvation experience when Jesus really showed up for you and changed your heart or circumstances.

- After you share your story, share the simple Gospel message in this practical way: "This was possible in my life because Jesus died on the cross for our sins, which separated us from the one true God. Jesus then rose from the dead, so He is alive today and waiting for relationship with us. He loves us! And do not forget to end with a question: "Is this something you are interested in? Do you want Jesus to change your life too?"

We can share anywhere, anytime, with anyone. We can share our Jesus-stories in just a short couple of minutes.

VARIOUS RESPONSES TO JESUS

What do we do with the various ways people might respond when we share?...

"I am ready to follow Jesus."

> Pray together with them right then! Say something like this to encourage them to begin a relationship with Jesus, "Why don't you pray out loud with me right now and tell Jesus something like this in your own words: 'Jesus, I believe You died on the cross for my sin and rose from the dead. Today I want to begin a relationship with You. I submit my life to follow You.'" (This concept comes from Romans 10:9.)

> Once someone believes in Jesus, begin going through this *Multiplying Movements* tool with them starting at Episode 1 so that they too can become a laborer for God's Kingdom!

"I do not want to follow Jesus. I am not interested."

> If someone is not ready to follow Jesus and not interested in learning more, then simply continue to love them in action, continue to share different stories of Jesus at work in your life as you get the chance, and most importantly keep praying!

"I'm not ready to follow Jesus yet, but I'm interested in learning more."

> You might find someone fumbling a little bit between being ready to follow Jesus and unsure if they are ready. If this is the case, you can ask a simple question like "What is holding you back from following Jesus?" and then discuss whatever that is.

It could be that this simple conversation removes their obstacle to following Jesus and they decide to believe!

In other cases, they might need more time before deciding to follow Jesus. If this is the case, ask them to begin meeting with you regularly to explore what Jesus is all about and discuss any questions they may have. Check out Appendix C - "Meeting with Those Interested But Not Ready to Follow Jesus."

NOW WHAT?

How does your perspective change, realizing that the Father, Son, and Holy Spirit are all inside of you, and that YOU are the extreme measure of God?

Jesus has always called His followers to proclaim what He has done in their lives, even from the very moment they encountered Him (see Mark 5:19-20). People who encounter Jesus most often experience some kind of change as a result (such as new peace, joy, freedom from a sin or addiction, hunger for God's Word, etc.).

Write down the three parts of your God-Story and combine them:

(Consider Reviewing the "Now What" section of Chapter 2, "The Starting Place: Developing a Heart on Fire")

Your life before God showed up:

How God showed up:

How your life was changed:

Practice your God-Story along with the basic Gospel message (cross and resurrection), and the ending question ("Would you like this in your life?").

Who will you share your God-Story and the Good News with, beginning this week?

Review your list of lost people from Chapter 2, "The Starting Place: Developing a Heart on Fire," and also consider others you have recently encountered in your life. Don't limit yourself to this list, but write it out as a strategic starting place.

1. _____ 2. _____

3. _____ 4. _____

5. _____ ...

BEGIN MEMORIZING THE MEMORY VERSE:

_____

". . . Pray that I may declare it fearlessly, as I should." — Ephesians 6:20, NIV

_____

WHAT IF . . . ?

Continue to share your God-Story with people on your list and with others week-by-week, along the way, wherever you go. As you do, God will begin to use you as the key to unlock people to the Good News of Jesus!

And as you engage lost people, do not forget that God may bring new people across your path that you could also take through *Multiplying Movements* to help them become true disciples of Jesus when they believe. It may be in your upcoming *Multiplying Movements* meetings. Or it could be later on. Remember, people are not projects but people to engage and people to love.

Send a reminder to your friends this week so they don't forget when and where you will be meeting. Confirm that they have ordered their book (or workbook), and ask them to register at MultiplyingMovements.com so they receive crucial Multiplying Movements elements and updates in their journey!

Let them know you are praying for them!

DISCUSSION

1. Share any victories or obstacles from last week's action steps.
2. Pray together.
3. Review Memory Verse.
4. Read Key Scriptures: Colossians 1:26-27; Mark 5:18-20; Acts 8:4.
5. Review key concepts from the chapter. Share how you are processing and any comments you have. Did anything in particular really resonate with you? Is there anything you

disagreed with? Or is there anything you will never forget? Do you have any questions about it?

6. The Father, Son, and Holy Spirit are all inside of you, and YOU are the extreme measure of God! How does this truth help you overcome any obstacle or fear you may face in sharing Jesus with others?

7. Each person, one at a time, practice sharing your God-Story. Share as if you are sharing with a lost person. If you are a large group, break up into pairs.

8. Again, each person, one at a time, practice sharing your God-Story as you would with a lost person, but this time include the Good News, and the ending question. After each person shares, pause to encourage and give feedback. In your feedback, make sure no crucial element was missed, whether the three parts of a God-Story, the Gospel, or the ending question.

9. Who do you plan to share with, starting this week? Of course, also recognizing that this is not to limit you but to be intentional to start. God may put an unexpected person in front of you at any moment, giving you an opportunity to share with them too!

10. Review "What If . . . " Section and the Memory Verse again.

11. Everyone share—what is your one key takeaway or action step for this week?

12. Pray together.

*Reminder: as you go to share your God-Story and the Good News, **begin by seeing, stopping, and spending time with people!**

OTHER HELPFUL RESOURCES:

Christian Man Laws (Book) by Adrian Despres

For purchasing options and more resources, go to:
MultiplyMore.com

NOTES
Reaching the Lost

EMBRACING GOD'S HEART FOR THE WHOLE WORLD

Matthew 28:17-20 • Matthew 24:14 • Revelation 7:9

**From the very beginning to the end,
God's heart has always been for the whole world, for all nations.**

OUR GOD-GIVEN PURPOSE

God had chosen Israel to be a Kingdom of Priests for _____
_____. (Exodus 19:6)

- Israel was chosen to _____ the one true God to the
  rest of the world.

- God desires for people from all nations to know and worship
  Him. (Isaiah 56:6)

- Yet, Israel failed to fulfill their God-given purpose. (Mark
  11:15-17)

. . .

In the Bible, the word _____ does not mean geo-political countries. Rather, it refers to tribes or ethno-linguistic people groups.

God has chosen us as _____ to proclaim Him to the world. (1 Peter 2:9)

STATS: THE STATE OF THE WORLD, MISSIONS, AND THE CHURCH

61% of Christians have never shared their faith (Lifeway Research)

42% of the world's population belongs to an unreached people group (3.14 billion people) ... (The Traveling Team Statistics)

- **Lost**: unbelievers who live in "Christianized" places are not unreached. They are lost.

- **Unevangelized**: unbelievers who are part of a people group or tribe with a Christian population higher than 2% but live in regions with absolutely no Christians, are considered "unevangelized."

- **Unreached**: a tribe/ethno-linguistic people group that is 0-2% Christian and has no ability to sustain Kingdom movement.

- **Frontier**: a people group with 0% Christianity.

- **Unengaged**: a people group with 0% Christianity, and no one attempting to bring the Gospel to them.

83% of the unsaved do not have access or opportunity to hear about Jesus. (The Traveling Team Statistics)

Of 400,000 cross-cultural missionaries only 3% go to the unreached. (The Traveling Team Statistics)

For every 1 unreached people group, we have 900 churches and 78,000 evangelical Christians... *There are roughly 7400 unreached people groups in the world! (The Traveling Team Statistics)

For every $100,000 of Christian income, only $1 goes toward initiatives for the unreached. (The Traveling Team Statistics)

51% of church attendees in the U.S. were unfamiliar with the term "Great Commission"...

> ... 25% or respondents said they heard of it but did not recall its "exact meaning" (Barna Research Group)

> ... That means that at least 76% of church attendees are clueless regarding God's burning passion for the unreached of the world!

The Great Commission: "Go make disciples of ____ _____."
–Jesus (Matthew 28:17-20)

- His final command must become our _____ concern!

- The Great Commission is not an option to be considered, but a _____ to be obeyed. –Hudson Taylor

---

WHY ARE WE FAILING TO FULFILL OUR GOD-GIVEN PURPOSE?

We may feel:

- Too inadequate.
- That we don't know _____.
- That Kingdom impact is for church leaders and _____ people.

    But, God can use _____ people to change the world! (Acts 4:13)

We might be:

- Too afraid.
- Lazy.
- Ignorant.
- Disobedient.

HOW DO WE ENGAGE GOD'S HEART FOR THE NATIONS?

3 Types of Christians (Romans 10:14-15)

- _____

- Senders

- _____

Which one are <u>you</u>?

A few ways you can participate as a *Sender*:

• _____.

• Give.

• _____ goers.

• Leverage your unique _____ and _____.

- *Business branch, platform, or name.*
- *Invent creative mission resources or mission technology.*
- *Use computer skills to help get the Gospel into restricted systems.*
- *Spread the story of God's Kingdom movement through photography and videography.*

A few ways you can prepare and participate as a *Goer*:

• Take a _____ _____ mission trip.

- *Be exposed to the unreached and great harvest needs.*
- *Build relationships.*
- *Share the Gospel.*
- *Discover what God is up to among the nations.*

• Research mission _____ that match you and your calling so that they help train and prepare you to launch out as a missionary to the unreached.

• Research and study other religions.

  - *Understand their beliefs.*
  - *Apologetics.*
  - *How to build bridges to their culture and beliefs.*
  - *Evangelism and discipleship tactics.*

• Find refugees and immigrants from unreached people groups near your city.

  - *Go meet them, build relationships, find ways to love them, and share the Gospel.*

• _____ for the unreached of the world and consider where God is sending you!

  - *Check out JoshuaProject.net and PeopleGroups.org (click on the interactive maps and look for the red dots – most unreached people groups of the world).*

  - *Prayerfully consider going to the most unreached places so that you can change the future of the statistics you discovered in this message!*

Jesus will build His Church,
even in the spiritually darkest places on the planet,
and He will not be _____!
(Matthew 16:13-20)

NOW WHAT?

Consider how you have engaged with God's heart for all nations up to this point. As of this moment are you living as a goer, sender, disobeyer, or some combination?

Brainstorm and write down some ways that you personally could more fully embrace God's heart for the whole world. Consider what skills, gifts, talents, connections, or resources you have that can be used to further God's mission, especially among the unreached who have never heard of Jesus.

Prayerfully Explore the Unreached People Groups of the World: Go to JoshuaProject.net and find the interactive map with dots showing people groups (Navigate to "Resources" and then click on Google Maps for "People Groups on Google Maps"). Explore the red dots in various countries and pray for them. Seek God for what He is asking you to do, to see more of the world reached!

Download the "Operation World" app to help you pray daily for the nations of the world.

The Unreached Near You:

Are there communities of refugees or immigrants within driving distance of your home? Do you live near a university or college campus with international students? Write them down here and begin to pray for them. Consider looking up organizations like ISI (International Students Inc.) to discover more opportunities to engage.

As you pray for communities of refugees, immigrants, and international students within driving distance of your home, prayerfully consider whether God might lead you to befriend them as a Kingdom Laborer, sharing your God-Stories, and even seeking to help them explore Christianity further by taking them through *Multiplying Movements.*

Are there any mentors, people, groups, or organizations in your life that could help you further understand and embrace your role in God's worldwide mission? What should you ask them? Write down your questions here and set up a time to meet with them or call them.

BEGIN MEMORIZING THE MEMORY VERSE:

—————————————————————————

"... Go and make disciples of all nations, baptizing them in the name of the Father and of the Son and of the Holy Spirit, teaching them to obey everything I have commanded you. And remember, I am with you always, to the end of the age." — Matthew 28:19-20, NIV

—————————————————————————

WHAT IF . . . ?

What if God used your life to create a domino-ripple effect that changed the future horizon of history globally! As you intentionally commit to live for Jesus, embracing His heart for all people in all places, He will do it! Never overlook anyone. God may have a plan you would never expect. As you come alongside one undervalued life, He may transform their life and send them to impact the world in places and ways you never imagined!

Remind everyone of your upcoming *Multiplying Movements* group or one-on-one time (likely starting next week)! For those who have not confirmed already, make sure they have ordered their book (or workbook) and registered for the *Multiplying Movements* journey at MultiplyingMovements.com:

Remind them: "Before each time we meet, we will each read the *Multiplying Movements* chapter (or watch the video) and personally process through the "Now What" and "What If?" reflection sections."

Additionally, begin to pray about where you could invest financially in God's global movement—especially among the unreached! While there are varying phenomenal places you could invest, you might consider what God is doing through Forge. Tens of thousands of people are coming to Christ among some of the most unreached and spiritually darkest regions of our world. Tens of thousands of Bibles are being distributed in some of the most restricted nations. Kingdom Laborers are being raised up, and lives are being changed one community at a time! Would you prayerfully consider furthering this movement? You can check out more of the global impact and give on the Forge website at ForgeForward.org.

DISCUSSION

1. Share any victories or obstacles from last week's action steps.
2. Pray together.
3. Review Memory Verse.
4. Read Key Scriptures: Matthew 28:17-20; Matthew 24:14; Revelation 7:9.
5. Review key concepts from the chapter. Share how you are processing and any comments you have. Did anything in particular really resonate with you? Is there anything you disagreed with? Or is there anything you will never forget? Do you have any questions about it?
6. What questions did you write down to ask a mentor?
7. Was there any particular region or people group that really stuck out to you as you explored the Joshua Project map and website?
8. How can you personally increase your engagement with God's heart for all nations?
9. Review "What If . . . " Section and the Memory Verse again.

10. Everyone share—what is your one key takeaway or action step for this week?

11. **Make sure to move into the next section, "Your Next Steps: Multiplying the Movement," either now or during one more final meeting next week.**

12. Pray together.

OTHER HELPFUL RESOURCES:

Mudrunner: Advancing the Kingdom No Matter the People, the Place, or the Cost (Book) by Charlie Marq

Fuel for the Harvest Podcast by Forge

For purchasing options and more resources, go to:
MultiplyMore.com

NOTES
Embracing God's Heart for the Whole World

YOUR NEXT STEPS: MULTIPLYING THE MOVEMENT

NOW IS THE TIME!

You have been equipped. This is just the beginning of your Laborership journey! Will you commit to becoming a Kingdom Laborer who spiritually multiplies others?

This is not just a close to a book study, but your ongoing launch into so much more! You are now equipped to live as a laborer and to come alongside others to help them discover the same Kingdom lifestyle you have.

You personally processed through each portion of Multiplying Movements. You have drawn near to Jesus and reached out to people all along the way. You have shared from your heart in discussion times. Every step you've taken was not just because of the person who took you through Multiplying Movements, but because of *your* initiative. You now have what it takes—with Jesus!

What matters most as you step forward is not your skills or abilities, but your willingness to say "Yes" to Jesus and His Kingdom cause.

And be encouraged, as you step out, one life will multiply into many. In Isaiah 51:2 God declares, ". . . I called [Abraham] when he was only one man, and I blessed him and made him many," or "I . . . multiplied him"(NIV). You are but one life. Others you come alongside are but one life. Yet, God will add the increase, turning one life into many and your impact will multiply!

So, will you—right here, right now, today—commit to fulfilling the prayer request of Jesus (Matthew 9:38) by living as a Kingdom Laborer *and* equipping others to do the same through Multiplying Movements? It is the very thing that Jesus has called us to (Matthew 28:19-20). You were made to multiply!

Check out the "Spiritual Multiplication Wheel" on the next page for a great visual of this!

Spiritual Multiplication Wheel

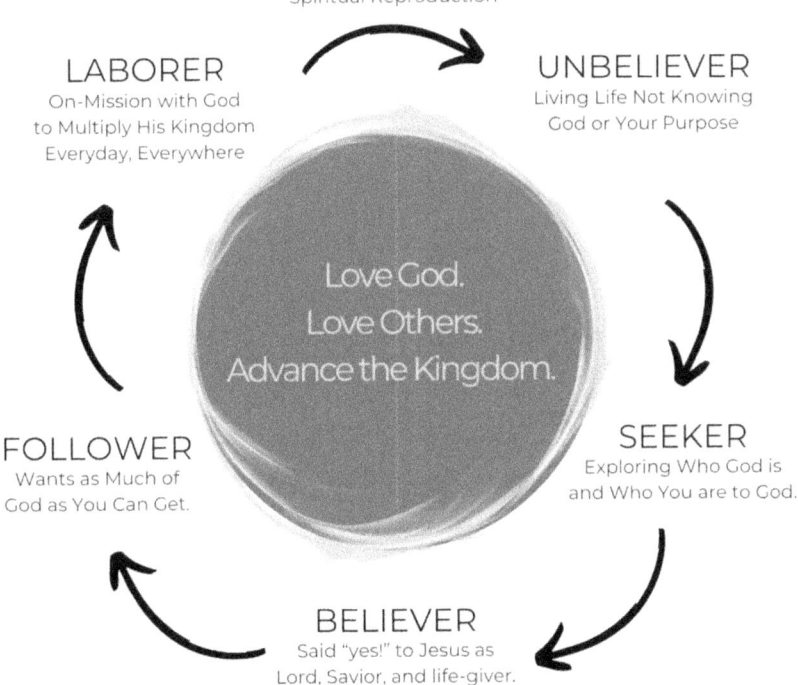

NOW WHAT?

You are probably launching your own Multiplying Movements meeting this week or next! Take a few minutes to write out any specific prayer requests you have for your group:

Read through "Appendix A – Tips For Coming Alongside a Person or Small Group" as you prepare to come alongside others using Multiplying Movements.

Read through and reflect on each point of "The Laborer's Declaration:"

THE LABORER'S DECLARATION

Kingdom Laborers are God's master plan for extending His love, grace, and truth to people everywhere. We, as everyday, ordinary people are His "Plan A" and there is no "Plan B!" Join the growing movement of Kingdom Laborers worldwide by making the following statements become declarations for your life.

You might consider placing these statements in a prominent location where you will frequently see them until they are displayed naturally through your life. Read and pray them often as you celebrate God's call and purpose for YOU to be His every day, everywhere laborer.

MY KINGDOM LABORER DECLARATION

1. I believe my life can become an answer to the world's greatest need, fulfilling Jesus' heart-cry for More Kingdom Laborers! From here forward, I will seek to live as Christ's "hands and feet" wherever I go.

2. Everyday, ordinary people just like me are God's master plan for reaching the world. With God's guidance and power, I will live a life of love as an active Kingdom Laborer.

3. As God is calling me to be a channel of His love and truth, I will intentionally see, stop, spend time, and share with people in the mainstreams of life—up-close, one life at a time.

4. While I do not have what it takes on my own to get over myself and into God's plan, "I can do all things *through Christ* who strengthens me" (Philippians 4:13)! Therefore, I will daily seek to love Jesus more—enabling the greatest gift I give the world around me to be my own intimacy with God.

5. God has designed me with a unique ministry purpose in mind. I will allow Him to employ my spiritual gifts, my passions, my talents, my personality, my strengths, my weaknesses, my experiences, my interests, my personal

tragedies, my past failures, my assets, and anything and everything else about me to minister to others.

6. I acknowledge that God has shown up in my life and therefore I have stories to share! I will make it my priority to point others to Jesus and His Good News as I share my God-Stories.

7. I believe ministry to others does not just happen as a planned event on my terms and in my timing. I will listen for and obey the Holy Spirit's "along the way" leadings, taking the opportunity to engage others in the ordinary moments and places of my daily life.

8. While the needs of the world are far too overwhelming for one individual, I recognize the power of spiritual multiplication. Therefore, I will fuel Jesus' growing Laborership movement, intentionally investing in others— one life at a time.

I choose to be God's Kingdom Laborer every day, everywhere!

Signature: _____ Date: _____

BEGIN MEMORIZING THE MEMORY VERSE:

— —

"And [Jesus] died for all so that those who live should no longer live for themselves but for the one who died for them and was raised." (2 Corinthians 5:15, CSB)

— —

DISCUSSION

1. Share any victories or obstacles from last week's action steps.
2. Pray together.
3. Review Memory Verse.
4. Share about your own upcoming *Multiplying Movements* group or one-on-one time: Who will you begin meeting with? Where and when?
5. Share the prayer request you wrote out for your upcoming group.
6. Together, read through and declare out loud the "My Kingdom Laborer Declaration" statements.
7. Pray over each other and commission each other as Kingdom Laborers, declaring over each person: "In the name of Jesus, we commission you to be God's every day, everywhere Laborer, and to multiply others to do the same."
8. Pray together.

Forge wants to continue to support you as you come alongside others using Multiplying Movements. Tell us about each new group you start at **MultiplyingMovements.com** so we can pray for you and connect you with additional resources.

We'll give you (and each person you come alongside) access to more Forge Resources, crucial updates, and encouragement in the journey! You will also get to continue being part of the greater Multiplying

Movements Laborership community and Forge Family where you can ask questions, share prayer needs, and connect with other Kingdom Laborers.

If you don't have a group of friends ready to start your own Multiplying Movements course, it's not too late! Read back through the "What If . . . ?" sections of each chapter, and start praying for and developing your group. God may lead you to meet with only one or two people, or maybe as many as twelve! He knows exactly what strategy will be best for you. Commit to let Him lead you.

APPENDIX A – TIPS FOR COMING ALONGSIDE A PERSON OR SMALL GROUP

INVITING OTHERS TO GO THROUGH *MULTIPLYING MOVEMENTS*

While there are example invitations scattered throughout the chapters, here is a general example that you can customize as needed and send as a text or email:

"[Name], you've been on my mind the last few weeks, and I think God is bringing you up for a reason . . . I have been praying for you!

I am inviting a few friends to get together to talk about God and His plan for our lives, and grow spiritually. I am looking at starting around [DATE]. Would you be interested in joining me?

We're planning to meet once a week over the next few months to really go deep and dive into the Bible together. We'll be using a resource called *Multiplying Movements*. I believe our lives will be deeply impacted as we go through it together!

I really hope you can join, but either way, I am super thankful for your friendship! Let me know what you think."

What if I run into snags or have questions?

As you begin coming alongside others, know that Forge is here to help you! If you have questions or run into snags, feel free to reach out to Forge at ForgeForward.org. You may also consider reaching out to whoever took you through *Multiplying Movements*.

If someone asks questions you don't have answers to, don't worry! It is ok to say "That's a great question and I'm not quite sure! Let's look into it this week and return to that question next week." Then over the week you could reach out to whoever took you through *Multiplying Movements*, reach out to Forge, or study further using sites like GotQuestions.org or CARM.org.

MULTIPLYING MOVEMENTS MEETING STRUCTURE (FOR ONE-ON-ONE OR A SMALL GROUPS)

Set a time to meet regularly (doing the same time weekly is highly recommended for consistency) for a recommended time of 75 minutes.

It will take at least 12 meetings or 12 weeks to go through *Multiplying Movements*. It may even take up to 14 meetings / 14 weeks if you want to take a week for the intro ("Don't Miss This: Your Launch Into the Multiplying Movements Vision") and a week for the outro ("Your Next Steps: Multiplying the Movement").

You can either read the chapters of this book **OR** utilize the *Multiplying Movements* videos with the video workbook. You can find and purchase all the videos and the accompanying video workbooks on the Forge App or at **MultiplyingMovements.com**. You have several options on how to incorporate the chapters or videos when coming alongside others, whether in a small group or one-on-one:

- *RECOMMENDED – BEFORE your meeting each week, have the group or person you are coming alongside read the chapter (or watch the episode) and process the "Now What?" and "What If . . . ?" sections at the end of each chapter, so that they are prepared to engage when you get together. Then, engage the "Discussion" section when you meet together.

- While it is NOT recommended, you might decide to watch the episode together. After watching, provide some space for each person to process the "Now What?" and "What If . . . ?" sections, and then go through the "Discussion" section together. Although it must be noted, this method will add significant time to your meeting and will likely be very difficult to do with several people on a consistent weekly basis.

- If you are watching the videos together, we recommend using the web version of the app, found at **MultiplyingMovements.com**, and watching on a larger device, such as a TV or computer. The "web version" page with a phone icon is a fully functional web version of the app. The videos can be played "full screen" once you start them.

- "Other Helpful Resources" are active steps mentioned at the end of each chapter (such as the Spiritual Gifts Test or the Spiritual Warfare message). These can be found at **MultiplyMore.com** or at **MultiplyingMovements.com** under "Looking for the recommended resources from Multiplying Movements?"

TIPS FOR FACILITATING DISCUSSION

When you begin the discussion each time you meet, ask each person to answer honestly, "Did you read the chapter or watch the episode for this week?" (so that everyone is held accountable to engage).

You will want to manage the discussion flow, keeping track of the start time and end time.

Be ok with some silent or quiet space in between questions to give people time to process (it can feel like an eternity, but even 45 seconds of silence is ok!)

If no one says anything for longer than that, then begin to prompt people with clarifying or follow-up questions. You can even ask, "Did you understand the question fully?" You could even share your personal answer to the question and then ask again, "So what about you?"

If someone is a bit quiet and needs some prompting to share, try individually inviting them to share from time to time: "Joe, do you have any thoughts on that question?"

Encourage participation and those who share by saying things like "Thank you for sharing that!" or "Wow, that is really powerful!"

If someone is dominating conversation, feel free to state something like "Thank you for sharing, Joe. Now, I would love to hear some more from those who have said less during our time." And then pivot to ask someone else their thoughts on the question.

If someone goes on way too long time in their sharing (more than 4-5 minutes), you can interrupt them and state something like "Joe, I appreciate all you are sharing, but want to provide enough space for everyone to share. So it may be helpful to keep our answers a little more concise."

If the conversation goes off topic, say something like "Hey that is a great topic for after our group discussion is finished. But, back on topic, what do you all think about . . . ?"

Freely ask individuals follow-up questions to help them process more deeply, such as:

- "Why do you think that is?" or "What do you think is behind that?"
- "What do you think God wants you to do with that?"

- ○ "What specific next step could you take to better live that out?"
- ○ "What do you think that would look like in your daily life?"
- ○ If someone shares generally about the topic but does not relate it to their own life (as they say something like "People are like this…" or "People need…" etc.), then you can ask them, "So based on what you just shared, how does that relate to your life specifically? Or what is God showing you individually in that?"

USING *MULTIPLYING MOVEMENTS* TO COME ALONGSIDE PERSONAL GROWTH, LABORERSHIP, AND SPIRITUAL MULTIPLICATION

For Their Spiritual Growth: As able, share a story or example of something from your life related to the chapter topic in order to challenge or encourage those you are coming alongside.

For Their Laborership: As laid out in the varying "Now What?" sections, encourage them to continue praying for and engaging lost people as they see, stop, spend time with, and share God-Stories. Ask them who they are praying for and who they are engaging.

For Their Spiritual Multiplication: When addressed in various "What If . . . ?" Sections: really encourage them to follow-through with the "What If . . . ?" challenges, and eventually to begin using *Multiplying Movements* to come alongside others in the same way they are receiving the content, letting them know they have what it takes! Ask them who God is leading them to come alongside to spend more time with.

WHEN YOU COMPLETE *MULTIPLYING MOVEMENTS* AND THE PEOPLE YOU HAVE BEEN COMING ALONGSIDE ARE CHALLENGED TO LAUNCH OUT ON THEIR OWN

For several weeks, check up on each person you took through *Multiplying Movements*. Ask if they have begun their group or one-on-

one meetings yet. Ask how you can pray for them. Encourage them to keep going!

If those who you took through *Multiplying Movements* are struggling to launch their own meeting or group, ask them what is holding them back or what their struggles have been. Listen to their obstacles, share some tips to help them overcome these obstacles, encourage them, and pray for them. Reach out to whoever took you through *Multiplying Movements* or to Forge if you need further help or tips in this.

Once those you took through *Multiplying Movements* actually begin to start their own meetings or groups, simply keep praying for them and be available when they reach out. Periodically reach out to encourage them and let them know you are praying for them!

Personally, start again! Ask the Lord who else He wants you to come alongside and begin the process to start a new *Multiplying Movements* group or one-on-one meeting.

Forge wants to continue to support you as you come alongside others using *Multiplying Movements*. Tell us about each new group you start at **MultiplyingMovements.com** so we can pray for you and connect you with additional resources.

We'll give you (and each person you come alongside) access to more Forge Resources, crucial updates, and encouragement in the journey! You will also get to continue being part of the greater *Multiplying*

Movements Laborership community and Forge Family where you can ask questions, share prayer needs, and connect with other Kingdom Laborers.

OTHER HELPFUL RESOURCES:

Baton Passing Relationships (Booklet) by Dwight Robertson

For purchasing options and more resources, go to:
MultiplyMore.com

APPENDIX B – STARTING A CHURCH (WHERE THERE ARE NONE)

Maybe there are no churches in your area, and therefore God is leading you to start one. In addition to what Chapter 6 outlines, consider these additional tips on launching a church gathering:

- It does not have to be complicated.
- Going through Multiplying Movements together could actually be how God leads you to start a church gathering.
- You can meet weekly in your home with just a few believers.
- Grow from there.

What do you do when you gather?

- You could consider starting by using the Multiplying Movements format and going through each week together.
- Provide opportunity for everyone to engage the practices of Acts 2:42.
    - Engage God's Word together (this could be teaching and discussion focused).
    - Pray together.

- ○ Remember the death and resurrection of Jesus together (communion).
- ○ Build meaningful relationships (that might mean you have meals together).
- Regularly encourage participation and allow space and time for various people to engage in the gathering (see 1 Corinthians 14:26).
- Regularly encourage believers to lovingly engage lost people in their everyday lives, eventually inviting them into the church when they come to believe or when they are willing to join.

APPENDIX C - MEETING WITH THOSE INTERESTED BUT NOT READY TO FOLLOW JESUS

Honestly discuss whatever questions or obstacles they may have. It is ok to say "I am not sure" to a question and come back to answering after some further studying. You might find GotQuestions.org or CARM (Christian Apologetics Research Ministry) to be helpful resources.

And when you meet, follow the order of the list of Bible stories below and discuss one passage each time you meet. Read the Bible story together and discuss it in this way:

1-What did you learn about God?

You can consider using these questions too: What did you learn about humanity? Or about evil? After discussing, you may also share about the theme of the story as outlined in parenthesis throughout the Bible Story Schedule.

2-If this story is true, how can you apply the story to your life?

The final story will lead them to an opportunity to believe in Jesus, after learning the overall story of the Bible.

Note: You might consider skipping some of the Old Testament stories after Creation and the Fall in Genesis 2-3 and going straight to Jesus in the New Testament (unless your context calls for more Old Testament stories upfront).

Bible Story Schedule: *

OLD TESTAMENT

Genesis 2:4-25 —

Creation: God's creation reveals His goodness and that He desires relationship with humanity.

Genesis 3:1-21 —

The Fall: Impact of sin on the world yet God still promises His provision, see especially verses 15 and 21.

Genesis 6:5-14; 7:1-5; 7:18-23; 8:1-3; 8:15-22 —

Noah: God's provision must be received.

Genesis 12:1-5; 22:1-14 —

Abraham: God's heart is for people of every nation and tribe in the world and God provides a sacrifice for the sin of them all.

Exodus 3:1-17 —

Moses: God sees and responds to the suffering of His people.

Daniel 3:8-30 —

Shadrach, Meshach, and Abednego: God is faithful and rescues His people.

---

* Inspired by Nyman, James. *Stubborn Perseverance.* Mission Network. December 2015.

NEW TESTAMENT

Matthew 1:18-25, Isaiah 7:14 —

The Birth of Jesus: The coming Savior for all the sins of the world.

Mark 4:35-41 —

Jesus calms the storm and He can calm all "storms" in our lives.

Luke 8:26-39 —

Jesus has power over darkness and evil spirits.

Mark 5:25-34 —

Jesus has power over sickness.

Luke 7:11-17 —

Jesus has power over death.

Luke 10:38-42 —

Jesus reveals what is most important in life: living up-close to Him.

Luke 10:25-37 —

Jesus defends the weak and teaches what is most important for His followers: loving God and loving others.

Mark 7:14-23 —

Jesus teaches what is sinful.

Luke 5:18-26 —

Jesus has power to forgive sins.

Mark 15:21-39, or 14:43-15:47 —

Jesus dies for our sins.

Matthew 28:1-10 —

Jesus rises from the dead and His followers worship Him.

John 9:1-7; 9:18-38; Romans 10:9 —

Jesus heals a man born blind and saves those who believe in Him.

At the end of the final story, discuss in this way:

"We see three responses to Jesus: 1) Deny Jesus like the religious leaders. 2) Believe secretly but not confess him like the parents. 3) Believe and confess Jesus publicly like the blind man. Who do you want to be more like, the religious leaders, the parents, or the man born blind?"

Based on their response, ask them if they want to follow Jesus and fully give their life to Him. If they say yes, then pray with them to begin a relationship with Jesus and begin going through Multiplying Movements together. If they want to believe but are afraid of publicly standing for Christ, still begin to take them through Multiplying Movements beginning with Chapter 1, if they are willing.

ANSWER KEY

Chapter 1 - The Vision: Becoming Kingdom Laborers
impact, close, mainstreams, life, See, Stop, Spend Time With, T I M E, perfect, worthy, God-stories, Christ

Chapter 2 - The Starting Place: Developing a Heart on Fire
1, Jesus, love, Bible, joy, used, love, puke, Christian, sin, sin, died, live

Chapter 3 - Seeking God Intimately
time, know, walked, lifestyle, please, know, Scripture, Prayer

Chapter 4 - Engaging the Word of God
friendship, obey, voices, truth, Head, Heart, Hands, Feet

Chapter 5 - Pursuing Passionate Prayer
practiced, Praise, Repent, Ask, Yield, suffering, sick, Passionately, specifically, faith, glory, Faith, promises

Chapter 6 - Participating in the Local Church
Church, Cornerstone, gathering, MY, souls, Teaching, Fellowship, Breaking of Bread, Prayer, scatter, gathering

Chapter 7 - Rediscovering the Good News
gospel, good news, separated, death, Jesus, dead, resurrection, resurrection, preaching, sin, every

Chapter 8 - Overcoming Hindrances
Unconfessed, Believing, truth, Bible, Unforgiveness, forgiveness, Unhealthy, Generational, Warfare, Jesus, enslaved

Chapter 9 - Walking by Faith
building, walked, reoccurrence, Scripture, I don't know, God, calculates, answer, leader, Jesus, God, Scriptures, Well done

Chapter 10 - Utilizing Your Unique Ministry
Ministry, serve, 160, abilities, Bible, whole, talents, hobbies, places, past experiences

Chapter 11 - Reaching the Lost
perfect, extreme measures, Fire, Whale, Seed, Christ, Holy Spirit, Father, inside, You, Christ

Chapter 12 - Embracing God's Heart for the Whole World
all nations, represent, nations, Christians, all nations, first, command, enough, up-front, ordinary, Goers, Disobeyers, Pray, Encourage, gifts, talents, short term, organizations, religions, Pray, overcome

MORE FORGE OPPORTUNITIES FOR YOU

ForgeForward.org

FORGE SPEAKERS & EVENTS
ForgeSpeakers.org

*Need someone to challenge your group to become passionate followers
of Jesus who live with hearts on fire and lives on purpose? Book a
Forge speaker for your next event!*

FORGE EQUIPPING PROGRAMS for ALL AGES
ForgeTraining.org

*Forge Equipping is not summer camp and training events "as usual."
Forge challenges and equips people of all ages to become unique,
lifelong Kingdom Laborers every day, everywhere.*

FORGE BOOKS & RESOURCES
ForgeResources.org

*Looking for a deeper relationship with God and practical ways to
widen His Kingdom impact through your life? Forge has the resources
you need.*

THE FORGE APP
Essential Kingdom Laboring tools right at your fingertips:
TheForgeApp.org

JOIN THE MULTIPLYING MOVEMENT
Where everyday followers become Kingdom multipliers:
MultiplyingMovements.com

DEVOTIONAL CONTENT FOR THE EVERYDAY LABORER
Subscribe to the Monumental Moments podcast and devotionals:
MonumentalMoments.info

FORGE VIDEO CONTENT
Subscribe to free video content:
Youtube.com/ForgeForward

FORGE PODCAST
FuelForTheHarvest.com

FORGE DAILY TEXTS
Scan the QR code or visit **ForgeForward.org/Sparks**
to join Spark of the Day
for one-sentence daily devotionals.

NEED PRAYER?
Email us at **Prayer@ForgeForward.org**

CONTACT US
14485 E. Evans Avenue
Denver, Colorado 80014
303.745.8191
info@forgefoward.org

Learn more and get involved at
ForgeForward.org

SUBSCRIBE TO FORGE
ForgeSubscribe.com

*Get the latest Forge news, weekly devotionals, and prayer updates all year
long to encourage you every day, everywhere.*

www.ingramcontent.com/pod-product-compliance
Lightning Source LLC
Chambersburg PA
CBHW070705130626
46553CB00005B/1841